Wonderful Ways
to Love a Child

Wonderful Ways
to Love a Child

Judy Ford

Conari Press
Berkeley, CA

Conari Press books are distributed by Publishers Group West
Printed in the United States of America on recycled paper

ISBN: 0-943233-89-5
Cover design and illustration by Christine Leonard Raquepaw

Library of Congress Cataloging-in-Publication Data

Ford, Judy, 1944-
    Wonderful ways to love a child / Judy Ford.
        p.   cm.
    ISBN 0-943233-89-5 : $9.95
        1. Parent and child. 2. Parenting. 3. Love, Maternal. 4. Love, Paternal. I.
Title.
HQ755.85.F68   1995
306.874—dc20   94-38252
                                                                                      CIP

For Amanda Leigh
who so graciously allows me
to share our story.

Acknowledgments

My appreciation to Mary Jane Ryan, editor-extraordinaire, for nudging me onward and upward—helping me find a way to share what I know.

My gratitude to William Ashoka Ross, who lovingly recorded the tales of our family and whose gentle presence remains in my heart.

And, last but not least, to the children and parents whose brilliance shines through these pages—thank you all.

Contents

❧ Expressions

❧ Esprit

Parenting with Loving Actions

*It is not enough to feel love for your child,
you must be able to express your love
through your actions.*

Loving your child is simple and perplexing—you can't just feel it, you've got to show it! Feeling love in your heart for your child is not enough—to love your baby, your toddler, your adolescent through all the stages and phases of childhood requires that you express your love through your loving actions; and, as you probably already know, it's a lifetime commitment that requires your energy, demands lots of work, and calls you to rise above your own conditioning and preconceived notions. You will have to grow to your highest calling. You will have to be always mindful of what you say and do, because you are the most important person in your child's life and in your heart you know that how you treat your child each and every moment does matter.

Your loving actions are needed from the instant you bring your baby into the world and forever after. Madeline and Dave take turns getting up at night, doing the laundry, cooking the meals, and changing the diapers. In just one month with a baby at home, their lives have changed considerably—no more sleeping in, no more leisurely showers, no more gourmet brunches or spontaneous outings. But as they put aside their own needs and desires to care for their newborn, Madeline and Dave are discovering that it is through their loving actions that their lives are enriched.

Quickly they are learning what many parents before them have learned—that you can't be selfish, self-centered, or lazy if you want to take loving care of your child; you will be called on to perform many mundane tasks of child rearing, many of which aren't all that fun, but when you do them anyway, because your child needs you to, you are taking right and loving action and the bond between you grows stronger. Madeline and Dave are learning, as you will too, that parenting requires continuous adjustment and loving actions, even when you are too tired to feel much love.

As a parent, a family counselor, and human relations consultant for more than twenty years, I have met hundreds of parents who've insisted, "I love my child," and although I believe they felt love, I sometimes couldn't tell it by their actions. Unknowingly and unintentionally they would criticize and undermine the child's spirit—it was as though they weren't paying attention to what they were doing. It wasn't that they were bad people, they just hadn't learned how to turn their love into daily action, hadn't put themselves in their children's shoes.

In the parenting classes I teach, parents continually ask how to create strong, nurturing families. They ask how to raise children with high self-esteem, how to laugh, lighten up, and have fun in the process. I meet hundreds of parents and children who desperately want to love and enjoy one another; and even though there are thousands of books on parenting filled with myriad tips and techniques, the parents I talk with want something different.

Perhaps because we are all so busy, tired, and overwhelmed by trying to be superparents that occasionally all that's needed is a gentle reminder of how to express our love to our children—of the loving actions we need to make.

Wonderful Ways to Love a Child is a guide for all parents who want to put love into action so they can give their children the very best start in life. It's a prescription to strengthen your family, packed with guidance and reassurance of what I know is possible. Use it daily for comfort and support, and it will empower you to be the kind of parent you want to be. It's filled with true stories from children and parents who are building strong, nurturing, loving families. Their stories can show you the way. Please remember these suggestions are not simple tricks; they must be used with integrity, compassion, and all the emotional honesty you can muster. If they are not truly part of you, they will not work.

As a parent, and a counselor of hundreds of others, I have come to see that the most important part of parenting is the quality of the relationship between you and your children—not what they wear, how they comb their hair, whether they finish in first, second, or third place, but rather how it feels to be together. When they are grown and have children of their own, none of you will remember their grades, but all of you will remember the quality of your relationship. My wish is that this book will give you some ideas for building a loving, lasting friendship with your children that will help them soar as individuals so that they will gladly come to visit as adults.

As a parent of a teenager, I know how important it is to be reminded of the loving relationship that can exist between parent and child and of the fun and excitement we can share in our homes. I offer this book as an invitation to keep growing in a positive, uplifting direction. Our pediatrician asked my daughter, Manda, at age four, "What do you want to be when you grow up?"

"A person," she answered.

Yes, it is so: A parent's calling is to raise a person. By making these loving actions part of your life, you have the power to build the kind of family unit most people long for. And together, if we learn to love our children well, we can save the world.

Essence

Parenting is a two-way street.
As you take them by the hand,
they will take you by the heart.

Really Love Yourself

ॐ ॐ ॐ

Loving yourself is the basis for all that is beautiful and meaningful in the human experience, and parenting is no exception. Simply put, because self-love is the basis of individual responsibility and joy, you cannot be a good parent if you don't love yourself. For it is through discovering how precious you are that you are able to have the courage and self-confidence that parenting requires; by loving yourself you will have an internal sense of well-being so that, rather than looking to your children for validation, you have your own identity. Loving yourself is the first step toward making room in your life for a new, little person, because you are then able to love your children for love's sake, rather than for what they can do for you.

What does it mean to love yourself as a parent? It means taking time for yourself daily. Respecting yourself. Pampering yourself once in a while. It means learning about your unique talents and enjoying whatever makes your heart sing. It means sticking up for yourself when you know you need to. It's a daily process in which you come to know yourself as you are, forgive yourself for the not-so-loving parts you uncover, and, finally, take whatever loving action is needed for your personal growth. When you love yourself you are able to admit your shortcomings, knowing that although things have not always been easy for you, you have done the best you can. When you love and accept who you are, you will not be afraid to grow, to learn, to change. You will feel alive and have the energy you need to enjoy and nurture your family. Because children learn by example, you are the greatest teacher of what loving yourself really means. Here's a story to illustrate:

Although Kris, age twenty-nine, felt guilty going back to college, she decided to follow her longing. The kids had to pitch in. They ate more fast food, had less money, and learned daily living skills earlier than some of their friends. At graduation her children, eight and nine, walked across the stage hand-in-hand with their mom. Upon her receiving her diploma, the kids handed her a handmade card that said, "We are proud of you! We did it." Think about the powerful, positive lessons Kris taught her kids by loving herself enough to follow her own heart: that success is possible, that success comes from teamwork, and that there is joy in pulling together.

If or when you find yourself feeling resentful toward your children, saying or thinking, "After all I do for you," it's time to shift the focus onto yourself. For when you are not true to yourself, instead of feeling love for your child, you soon start resenting him or her, and that wall of resentment is hard to take down. When you are not true to yourself, you feel out of balance and your day gets out of whack; you get angry more quickly and snap more. But when you take care of yourself, your children feel contentment in their bones.

Allow Them to Love Themselves

A little person who loves himself grows up to be a responsible adult, able to live life fully. High self-esteem is the best foundation for your children's future. Experts in child development tell us that when children have high self-esteem they are able to learn and function better in school, they have friends, they feel connected with others, and they know they belong. They are competent, can make meaningful decisions, and are willing to try. They are optimistic, curious, and enjoy life. Loving oneself develops true character that cannot be swayed by such things as peer pressure or the countless outside influences your child will surely face.

Helping your children accept themselves just as they are is what unconditional love is all about. So above all else, don't base your love on what they do, but rather simply on the fact that they exist. When Garret asked his dad, "What do you like about me?" his father answered, "You!"

"What about me?" asked Garret.

"What I like about you, Garret, is that you are you. I like you."

One day when my daughter, Manda, was in the first grade, she came home from school and I asked her, "What did you do in school today?"

"I can't tell you," she announced.

"Why not?"

"Because you'll get mad."

Now, of course, I was more curious than ever. So I thought about it for awhile and then told her, "Manda, if you decide to tell me what you did in school today, I promise that if I get mad, I'll just go straight to my room."

"You promise?"

"Yup," I replied.

"Well, today we had to write down who our best friend was. . . . I didn't write down you, Mom."

"Oh?"

"I wrote down me. I just can't help it, I like me best! But I wrote you down second."

I was so pleased; I thought to myself, congratulations, you haven't ruined her yet. I was glad that she liked herself first and that she recognized her own value, because with this inner sense of self-worth, I knew she would enjoy herself, her school, her friends, and her life.

When a little person finds herself through the miracle of self-acceptance, her life becomes a self-fulfilling journey; suddenly she's powerful enough to bravely cope with all the challenges and the ups and downs that life will bring. The bonus is, as she learns to be compassionate toward herself, love for others is sure to follow.

11

Learn About Parenting

❀❀❀

If you have ever rocked a baby in the stillness of the night, then got up with the light of morning exhausted from lack of sleep, you know how difficult parenting can be and also what joy your child can bring. If you have ever cuddled your baby and had that very same sweet-smelling baby spit up on your freshly washed shirt, you know how frustrated you can feel while at the same time your heart wells up with overwhelming love. If you have ever resented spending your hard-earned money on piano, tennis, swimming, ballet, or gymnastics lessons that seem to be taken for granted, then watched with pride your child's sense of accomplishment, you know the difficult journey you face and what rewards it will bring.

Sometimes you get so annoyed that you want to scream, rant, and rave about all you have done for them; then they bring you a bouquet of dandelions and your heart melts. As they grow they seem to challenge you at every turn—they no longer accept your guidance unquestioningly, but seem to disagree with every word you utter; then when you're sure you'll go mad, out of the blue they make an observation, see a new angle, or put a new twist on things, and you marvel at the brilliance of their perspective.

No one ever said parenting is easy. Parenting means giving unselfishly when you are exhausted. It means buying your children new shoes while you go without. It means going by someone else's schedule. It means staying up late and not being able to sleep in. It means sharing everything— your money, your food, your makeup, your socks. It means looking out for another's welfare. When your children are babies it seems as though you pack up the entire house just to go to the grocery store, and when they are older you drive them to the movies, but they won't sit next to you. Some days they won't leave your side, but other days, without knowing how, you embarrass them, and they refuse to be seen with you in public. You strive to be a good parent, but you struggle with self-doubt.

Although parenting is perhaps the most important calling, it is the least-taught art in this culture. As a society we seem to think that the mere biological capacity to bear children qualifies us to raise them well. But we are slowly recognizing that we could all use some lessons, some skill building, and fortunately there are many great classes around. Parent Effectiveness Training is an wonderful course taught almost everywhere, or look for classes at your local community college; talk to other parents, or read books on parenting and child development. You might consider joining or starting a parenting support group, or taking a class to help you heal and grow. If you are not happy with yourself and who you are as a person, you can't give to your child what you don't have yourself. Perhaps you might benefit from counseling. Whatever your need, if you look, you will find it; if you need help, please ask for it.

Handle with Care

❧❧❧

When a package arrived in the mail marked "handle with care," no one would consider throwing it around carelessly. No one would ignore it, regard it as a nuisance, or be annoyed with it. The package would be opened slowly, tenderly, because it is fragile. Loving attention would be given. Perhaps if we think of children as precious little bundles sent special delivery directly from the heavens, we might be more patient with their troublesome behaviors.

Our children do many things that frazzle our nerves and push our buttons, but remembering that their hearts are delicate might help us be more sensitive. It is possible to devastate children's spirits with harsh words, or by ignoring them, or brushing them off. So instead of threatening, "If you don't stop it this minute, I'll really give you something to cry about," or asking the ridiculous, "Do you want a spanking?" try stopping for a moment to ask yourself, Why am I overreacting?

There is a big difference between acting and reacting, and as a parent it is important to learn the distinction. This requires thought, practice, and a lot of deep breathing. When Tommy broke his mother's favorite vase after she had asked him repeatedly to stop throwing the ball in the house,

14

for a moment she thought she would come unglued. She didn't react; instead she counted to a thousand and waited to see what would happen. She told me she learned a lot that day: Tommy had to focus on his own misbehavior instead of dealing with her hysterical reaction. He quietly picked up the broken vase and brought it to her, and she could see that he had learned a painful lesson. They talked about what had happened, and he promised never to throw the ball in the house again. And he didn't.

When you find yourself coming down hard on your child, or when your reaction is out of proportion, take a long deep breath, count to ten or ten thousand, and ask yourself, "What is going on with me, right now?" or "Why am I feeling this way? Breathe, breathe, breathe, and think before you act, so that once again you can feel the extraordinary sweetness of your child. Nothing is more important than handling their bodies and souls with tender loving care.

Give Your Presence

✿✿✿

Being present is making contact with the essence of the other person. It is meeting your child in the moment, without concern for the past or the future, and with your mind emptied of distractions. This means you come to your child free of expectations, preconceived notions, and the thousand other things you "need" to be doing, so that you can focus completely on his or her needs. This is not always easy, but it is vitally important.

Do you remember hearing stories of the poor little rich kid who had every material advantage but whose heart was broken because the parents were never really there? Sadly, there are many children who suffer from this kind of neglect. Gifts, no matter how expensive, will never take the place of your presence. Giving your complete attention is much more valuable to a growing child and is the most satisfying way of being together.

As an infant your child requires your presence constantly, but as she gets older it's easy to forget to pay attention, so watch for signs that she may be feeling abandoned. Perhaps her pestering you while you're on the phone is a signal that she needs more undivided attention. Once a six-year-old boy told me that the only time his father paid any attention to him was when he got in trouble at school and, since he wanted his dad's attention, he didn't mind the trouble. I suggested to his father, Don, that he spend a half-hour each evening just hanging out with his son. He wasn't sure it would make a difference but agreed to try. The trouble in school stopped, and Don discovered how important his presence was to his young son.

As kids move toward independence, you will be more on top of their adventures if you tune in without distraction. Amber, for example, schedules Saturday-morning breakfast dates at a neighborhood cafe with her nine and eleven year olds. She finds that just an hour away from home to focus on their needs keeps the lines of communication open.

Children do not always communicate with words, so be aware of the nonverbal ways children try to get you to listen. Hailey, at age five, started sucking her thumb again, whereas Ian was always so excited to talk with his parents at dinnertime that he could not eat. Davey complained of a stomachache each morning before school, and Candice bit her fingernails or twisted her hair when her parents argued. A child who repeatedly cries when left with a baby-sitter or clings and whines when with other adults may be sending a message that you need to be paying more attention.

Clear your mind, clear your schedule, and really be there. When you can't give your full attention, tell them so, then schedule a time when you can—and keep it. Turn off the television and turn on the answering machine. Sit together, talk, relax and unwind, and you will feel the connection grow stronger. If you are truly present when you are together, when you're apart they will rest assured your love surrounds them.

Listen from Your Heart

❧❧❧

Listening from your heart is completely different from listening with your ears. Few people know how to do this, and very few parents listen to their children this way. Listening from the heart means being genuinely interested, open, and caring. It means being eager to hear, to learn, to be astonished—without the need to argue, interrupt the flow, or give advice (the really hard part!). Listening from the heart means not jumping in with your point of view, but rather hearing what life is like from your child's perspective. It is listening with a sense of wonder. When you listen from your heart, your child feels safe to tell all, for a child who is with a receptive adult opens up and shares freely.

When Jake was caught cutting high school, he was upset and called his dad, John, insisting he pick him up right away. While driving to the school John reminded himself not to jump to conclusions but to allow Jake to do the talking. Jake told his dad that he didn't want to return to school that day, that he needed time to think. So instead of scolding, lecturing, or dispensing advice, John took his son for a walk and continued listening. Jake talked about everything from soccer to grades to money. The more John listened, the more Jake shared. He talked about his girlfriend, sex, and his future. Because of John's heartfelt listening, what might have been a confrontation softened into an intimate father-son conversation, ending with Jake listening to his father's point of view.

A child who is upset needs sensitive listening where few words are exchanged. Remember that saying "Oh" or "Hmmm" is sometimes enough; the fewer words from you, the better. Don't try to coax for more information than your child wants to give. Crystal cried and gasped for air while she told her mother how Lissy wouldn't share the dolls. Fortunately, Mom avoided the tendency to fix the problem. She listened, nodded in understanding, and, as often happens, within an hour or so Crystal was playing with Lissy again.

A child who is crying does not want to be asked questions or be given advice. In fact, he wants you to understand without his having to explain. When your child has finished crying or is no longer so upset, you might ask a simple question, such as, "Something happened?" or "Bad day?" Too many questions and your child feels defensive. Some children will share more; others will want to keep it to themselves, and you need to learn to respect their way.

Listening from your heart will heighten the sense of closeness with your child, and many times you'll discover that your gentle, quiet listening is all that's needed for your child to find his own solution.

Speak Kindly

❧❧❧

Like adults, children respond well to kindness. While what you say and the tone of your voice indicates how *you* are feeling, your child will interpret your words and tone as direct messages about his own self-worth. So speak gently and kindly, and your children will listen. There's no need to sound like an old shrew to get their attention.

Stop yelling. Shouting at children or to your spouse creates tension in the air, bad vibes around the house, and noise pollution in your head. It is not a good idea. Don't preach, nag, lecture, or pontificate either. Stop all the harping and blaming. Drop all criticism either direct or disguised. Don't bully, scream, call names, or threaten. For some of us, this is much easier to say than to do. We grew up in families that screamed and shrieked, blamed, and poked fun at one another, so it feels almost natural to do it. I suggest to parents with that kind of history that they stop before the harsh words come out and ask themselves, "If this child were me, how would I like to be spoken to?"

Maggie was worried sick when Joel, eight years old, who was supposed to be playing at the neighbor's, could not be found. She searched high and low, called everyone, and yelled for him. By the time he came walking up the street two hours later, she was in tears. She was so relieved she wanted to hug him, scold him, take him in her arms, and threaten him so he would never do that again. Wisely, instead she gently took his hand, walked silently for a block, and then asked, "Where were you, Joel?"

"Didn't you get the message on the answering machine?" he replied. "Ben's dad took us to play basketball. We saw a dog get hit by a car and took it to the vet."

She listened quietly as Joel told the story in great detail, sometimes fighting back his tears. She was so glad that she had held her tongue before she spoke, and so glad she had listened instead of talking so much as she sometimes did. When she got home, sure enough, just as she had taught him to do, there were two messages on the machine, letting her know what was happening.

When you find yourself becoming overwrought, take time to unwind—go for a walk or call a friend. Clear your head first, then, when you're ready, talk things over. Remember, every interaction has tremendous potential to hurt or heal, to wound or inspire. And in the midst of chaos your simple act of kindness can turn their day and yours around.

Encourage, Encourage

❦❦❦

We all need encouragement—you do and so does your child. In some ways we are all helpless little people trying to cope with a complex world. The rules change practically every day and it's hard to keep up. No one needs encouragement more than children. There are so many pressures and temptations that they need all the support we can give. Whatever they try to do, stand behind them. Let them know you believe they can accomplish their goal by saying, "I think you can do it." Acknowledge their accomplishments, however small.

Be careful not to confuse encouraging with pushing. Too often I see parents who are actually *discouraging* their child by pushing the things *they* care about rather then letting the child fulfill his or her own desires. For example, Sloane wanted her daughter Lindy to excel in track, and daily pointed out her talent. She was quite surprised when Lindy quit the track team and told her, "If you like track so well, why don't *you* do it?" Sloane had to admit that she was pushing her favorite sport rather than supporting Lindy in doing what *she* wanted.

Don't try to persuade your child to follow your dreams by saying, "I'd rather you become an engineer," to her desire to become an editor.

When you encourage, you inspire your child to be herself. If she has a dream, tell her it's a wonderful dream—no matter what. Don't knock it and don't put fear into her by saying, "There aren't that many jobs for astronauts."

Children have goals and ambitions of their own. Your job is to cheer them on. And don't forget to recognize their efforts. One parent said after reviewing a much improved report card, "You put in a lot of work to get these grades. Congratulations!" In some families the child who messes up gets all the attention, so don't forget to give words of praise to the child who is quietly doing well.

Suzannah frequently says to her children, "I trust you to know what is right for you." Such heartening words are music to the ears and echo the message: It's okay to discover who you are and to find out what you're all about. With such uplifting coaching from you, even when they have a setback, they won't be pessimistic for long.

Love them and believe in them totally. Jean and George told their children, "Whatever you are wishing for, we wish for you." With this kind of loving backup, you will be a light of inspiration guiding your children as they become what they are capable of being.

Try to Understand

❧❧❧

Children crave parents who understand them. Whether they are learning to ride a bicycle or cooking breakfast for the first time, your children are mastering new skills and need you to understand that life is also difficult for *them*. If you understand your child, he will feel safe to come to you. When life shuffles and tosses your children around, they will find solace and protection in the shelter of your understanding: "I know you're disappointed—tell me all about it." As Courtney said, "My parents may not always agree, but they always try to understand."

Understanding means not only that you understand what they are saying, but also that you are aware of when they are down, need to be left alone, or are hurt or frustrated, even if they don't say so with words. Nine-year-old Seth came home and, as usual, went straight for the refrigerator, but his mother noticed something wrong; perhaps it was the deliberate way he walked or the hang of his head.

"Are you upset?" she asked. When he denied it, she didn't question further, saying, "Well, just the same, please go easy on yourself." As he left he nodded. Later he told her he was having trouble with some kids at school, but he appreciated her knowing "when to stay out of my head." It made him feel he could solve his own problem.

Understanding is not jumping to conclusions, thinking you know for sure what is going on. Try to understand the meaning behind the words. When Leon, age five, dropped his ice-cream cone on the ground and started sobbing, his mom said, "Don't cry—I'll get you another one." She was puzzled when he insisted he didn't want any more ice cream. When he went off to sit by himself, she realized he had spilled the ice cream on his favorite baseball shirt.

"Are you worried about your shirt?" He nodded. "Are you worried that the stain won't come out?" He shook his head. "Are you worried that it won't be clean by tonight?"

"Yup!"

By coming to this understanding they were ready to find the solution.

Understanding means letting your child be in charge and not quickly taking over. A child learning to tie his shoes may get easily frustrated, but even so he does not want you to do it for him. Instead suggest, "You might try it this way." When your child asks for your advice, don't rush in with your answers so quickly; instead ask, "What do *you* think?" This gives him confidence to solve his own dilemmas. He relaxes, tensions melt away, and he is able to accept the challenge of the task at hand.

Answer Their Questions

✿✿✿

If you want the kind of relationship with your child in which he knows he can come to you with any question, concern, or upset, be sure to answer his questions honestly. This is not always easy, because children have a knack for asking the hard ones: "Did you ever skip school?" "What happens when you die?" "Who is God's mother?"

Constant questions are a sign of an intelligent child. And it isn't a sign of disrespect when she questions your words or actions. An inquisitive child does not go along willy-nilly with authority figures, including her parents. A child who follows blindly without asking why can be easily led. So respect questioning. And if you don't know the answer, say so—"I don't know, that's a good question"—then help your child find answers. Try not to lose patience with the continual "whys" or "how comes" the little ones ask, nor with the tougher questions that are sure to follow.

When Megan asked her mom if she had ever smoked cigarettes, Karen wanted to stretch the truth but decided to be straightforward rather than have Megan find out from Grandma, and perhaps, she thought, Megan might already know. So Karen answered yes, which led to an open talk between them. Remember that lies, half-truths, and deceptions confuse a child. No matter how tough the question, the truth is always better. If you avoid giving honest answers, your child will get the feeling that she can't trust you.

Here's the tricky thing about questions: although it is important to *answer* their questions, it is equally important that you not *ask* too many yourself. Perhaps you've noticed that children, especially as they approach their teens, often get defensive when you ask even the simplest question. Though you are genuinely interested in their lives, they for some reason think you are snooping, prying, or butting in where it is none of your business. Teens share only what they want, when they want. So here is the rule: Don't ask teenagers many questions, but *always* answer theirs. You can survive with your sense of humor intact if you think of it as a stage they're going through, albeit a long one! This too shall pass, and you will once again be able to have a normal conversation.

Ask Their Opinions

Raising children is a two-way street. It isn't just the filling up of an empty vessel with your thoughts, feelings, and beliefs. Kids have opinions, impressions, thoughts, and ideas of their own to share, if you would just ask. And if you are willing, they can even show you a new perspective. They tell the truth. We adults may be a little jaded, or perhaps we have forgotten what it's like to be a child. Molly told her father as they were getting ready for church, "It's hard to go to church when I'm having fun at home."

Children have opinions about a lot of things. Take the time to say, "What do you think?" or "I'm wondering how you are feeling," or "Any ideas?" Listen to their responses. From something as simple as what to cook for dinner to the more complicated matters of allowance and curfew, children have valid suggestions and observations of their own. Michelle proposed painting her room pink, yellow, and green plaid. It looks great! Even very young children know what they like. At ten months old, Martin knew for sure that he didn't like squash and spit it out each time his father tried to feed it to him, and one-year-old Kalle hated playing in sand or getting her hands dirty.

Children are curious observers of their world. Let them know it's okay to express themselves. You might be surprised at what they have already learned. Lacey told her aunt, "My mom thinks there's a Santa Claus, but I know there isn't." At six years old, Jill told her mother, "I'll study my spelling words after I play for one hour." And Riley told his parents, "I think playing one sport is enough for me."

Children have lots to say and when asked will give you new ideas where you might be stuck. At age eight, Manda told me about a new baby-sitter and got her phone number from a neighbor. We tried her out and Manda informed me, "She isn't any good because she talks on the phone too much." So I didn't use her again.

Don't be so quick to discount your child's thoughts and feelings. Recently, while speaking to a group of junior high students, I asked them what they wished their parents would do differently. One girl raised her hand and said, "I wish my parents would listen more." Several others agreed, and one teenage boy added, "Kids know how to listen better than adults."

Kids do have something to say, so if you stay open to what that is, you will discover what they know. Involving your child in this way may take time and energy, but it's the beginning of creative problem solving.

Learn from Them

❧❧❧

Children have a fresh point of view, and if you choose to, you can learn from them. The old philosophy that parents always know what's best is not necessarily true. Although it might be a blow to our egos to acknowledge that we are still learning, our children will respect us when we do.

Not all parents find this easy to do. Bruce was from the old school—he wanted his daughter to be a lady and would not give her permission to play sports. She rebelled and secretly joined the tennis and basketball teams. When he first found out he was angry, but when he attended her tournament and saw her skill, her effort, and the recognition she earned, he bravely acknowledged he had been wrong. Don't be afraid to admit when you don't know something. You won't lose credibility when you say honestly, "I don't know," or "I'm not sure about that."

Every parent can learn something valuable from a child. When Paige became involved in her ten-year-old son's science project, he showed her the importance of recycling, so together they started recycling at home. From computer games and fashion trends to the newest slang and how to use a VCR, we can always learn something new, even if, as we get older, it seems we don't catch on so quickly.

To keep learning, stay curious about the world. To be connected with your child, be inquisitive about their world. Watch and learn. Richard, a father of three boys, studies occasionally with his sons just to stay in touch with how things have changed. "History has been made and written since I was in school," he says. "Textbooks are different."

Learning from a child sends the message, "I am glad you're growing up." As your child grows, he will go through many changes, stages, and phases. It will be easier if you stay flexible. Adjust your attitudes and rules and let them guide you. Don't be so set in your ways. When a big person says to a child, "Maybe you're right," or "I never looked at it that way," or "I see what you mean," their spirits naturally soar.

Say Yes as Often as Possible

Yes is one of the most important words you can use with your children. Say yes to them so they can say yes to life. A child raised with yes feels positive about himself and the world awaiting. A child who has been given the go ahead to explore her world learns to be naturally optimistic and a self-starter. "Yes children" are naturally motivated and believe they can make things happen. They are willing to find out and take charge. Unfortunately some parents are fearful, thinking it is better to control the child with *no*—they automatically say no to everything; but this approach soon backfires. A child raised with lots of noes is defeated before he starts. He feels frustrated and, in extreme cases, hopeless. He stops trying, gives up, and becomes depressed. He has sad eyes.

Teens, especially, need lots of yes. I try to look at it this way: a child asks for whatever she is ready to handle. You never hear a five year old asking to drive a car or go to a dance. Even preteens start asking for more privileges because they are ready for the responsibility associated with this new adventure. They are ready to expand their world, and when you say yes you are sending a positive message that you trust them, and that in turn helps them become more independent and trustworthy.

I'd like to point out, however, that there is a big difference between saying yes so that your children see life in a positive way and saying yes indiscriminately, allowing them to do anything. Overly permissive parents give the go-ahead by default, because it's easier than taking an active interest in their children's activities; on the other hand, responsible parents know what's going on and say yes because they understand that the experience will be beneficial. Overly permissive parents give the impression of not really caring, whereas "yes parents" watch closely as they allow their children to expand their boundaries.

When children ask, give them a positive, affirmative reply. And if you can't say yes right away, try, "Sounds interesting—let's talk about it," or "I'd like to think that over." Yes opens the doors of possibilities and the windows of opportunity. Yes creates an atmosphere of cooperation and excitement. It makes the world a friendlier place. Yes lets your child move out into the world and explore.

Say No When Necessary

Of course there are times when you must say no. As a child grows and learns about himself, he needs to know the guidelines for his behavior and will look to you for direction. You must be willing to set the limits: you can't jump on the furniture, you must be with an adult if you want to light the fire, no more television tonight, you have to buckle up in the car, hold my hand when we cross the street.

Setting boundaries is different from punishment. Punishment is the infliction of pain, which never teaches the child anything except negative emotions of fear and hate. There is never any need for punishment. Blaming, threatening, lecturing, and controlling also don't work; they lead to unnecessary power struggles. Instead of being an authoritarian dictator, think of yourself as a compassionate coach communicating the necessary rules—this is how we play the game and this is why.

A nurturing parent says no in a clear, honest way, finding the right time and taking care not to shame or embarrass. Some parents tend to lecture when saying no. Alan and Kate told their son no to a request he had made, and then continued with a long explanation and lecture, hoping perhaps he would understand or appreciate their reasoning. He looked at them and said, "Lecturing is not going to make me like your decision." He did not need a lecture on top of the no. Saying no without lots of explanation helps you avoid the pitfalls of endless, needless arguing.

To be able to say no appropriately, you must practice emotional honesty, which means following the same guidelines yourself that you set for your children. Dave swore like a crusty sea captain and then wondered why his four-year-old son did the same. Your children will follow your example, so if you don't want swearing, don't swear yourself. That is being congruous and honest with your rules.

Use your no as a gentle tool for teaching and guiding. Thoughts, feelings, and wishes are okay, but undesirable behavior is not. Avoid being overly permissive, allowing your children to do whatever they please. When your children are misbehaving, they need your help to get themselves under control. Strive for agreeable limits and creative individualized solutions. You are not being mean when you discipline this way—you are doing your child a service. Remember that the goal of discipline is self-discipline. Children feel an inner freedom and security knowing they have learned to guide themselves—a strength they will surely need to be fully functioning adults.

Honor Their Noes

I am sure you have noticed that two year olds spend a whole year saying no to everything. Sometimes it is the very first word they utter. This can be frustrating if you don't understand the significant purpose behind it.

Saying no is the first way a child asserts himself as an individual and is a sign that he is grasping the concept that he is a separate person from you. Saying no is the first way a child feels powerful. It begins around age two and surfaces again ferociously in the teenage years. This is perfectly natural. You can relax when you remember that sometimes no just means "not now" or "I'm not ready." At two and a half, Parker insisted on picking out his own clothes. He absolutely would not wear overalls, even though that's practically all he owned. He decided that he hated them, and that was that! Rather than get involved in a power struggle, his mother decided to see it as an act of maturing; after all, she certainly didn't like being told what to wear either. Respecting their no, even when it doesn't seem logical to you, lets your child practice his independence, learn that he can influence things.

Remember to appreciate the nonverbal noes as well, by respecting their privacy and giving them physical and emotional space. This means no snooping in diaries, rummaging through drawers, listening to phone calls, or reading their mail. I learned the hard way when I read my daughter's yearbook inscriptions without her permission. She was mad at me and rightly so. I was wrong for being so nosy. Sometimes you can turn a no into a yes by admitting you are wrong. The following year I was surprised when Manda voluntarily let me read her yearbook.

One way to avoid endless nos from your child is to give him choices like, "Would you prefer to take out the garbage or set the table?" or "Will you mow the lawn Friday night or Saturday morning?" Allow your child control over his world by giving plenty of choices and you'll have fewer noes.

A child who trusts you to respect his independence has little need to rebel. The most rebellious and depressed adults are those who, as children, were the most strictly controlled. They were not allowed to find their own identity or make their own choices. Right or wrong, they were forced to dutifully follow their parents' authority.

Respecting your children's separateness from you means you won't snoop, meddle, coax, pry, or listen in, and it means you let them practice saying no in the house, so that they will be ready when temptation comes around. Away from home, they will need this personal power.

Celebrate Mistakes

❧❧❧

Children aren't afraid of trying something new, and they aren't afraid to fail and try again. Why, then, are we adults so often hung up on failure—ours and our kids'? Why is it so hard to let our children be average or make mistakes? Why are we so anxious whenever our child goofs up?

Perhaps you suffer from the unconscious belief that it is vital to your well-being and success to always look good and always do things right. Perhaps when something goes wrong you feel you have failed. Sometimes parents' expectations are so high that children give up before they start. Your own fear of failure might be inhibiting your children from doing their best, for mistakes are the cornerstones on which we build success.

Experts in motivation tell us that it is our *attitude* toward mistakes that makes the difference in reaching our goals—not the mistakes themselves. However, some parents cannot tolerate the notion that making mistakes is part of the process. You've probably witnessed parents at a sporting event freaking out and yelling stern instructions from the sidelines. You felt so sorry for the kids and wondered what was going on inside the parent that made the child's batting average a matter of life and death.

If you're forever scrutinizing every detail of your child's performance, he is likely to become a frustrated perfectionist which, in the long run, leads to burnout. Julia went to great lengths to ensure that her son Mark excelled. She rewarded high grades with money and restricted his play when he messed up. Each year he found it harder and harder to meet her expectations, and whenever he failed, he called himself "stupid."

Although making a mistake can be disappointing, it's not a catastrophe, and it's important that your children know the difference. A scientific study demonstrates why: Two groups of students were taught new math problems and new spelling words early one morning. Then they were given a snack break and time for visiting or further study; the break was followed by an exam. This pattern continued throughout the day. Some startling discoveries were made: (1) the spelling words and math problems that stuck with the students the longest were the ones they missed the first time, and (2) the students who were scolded and made to study harder continued to get worse scores while these who were pleasantly guided to learn from their mistakes showed continual improvement.

We all make mistakes, but the winner knows that success comes from perseverance: trying, failing, learning, and doing it again until he succeeds. Most important, a winner does not waste energy by scolding or berating himself. He keeps practicing, takes a break, and tries again. When you shift the emphasis from trying to avoid mistakes to celebrating the knowledge gained, children remain willing to try, try again.

Admit Your Mistakes

❧❧❧

As parents we have made all kinds of mistakes; we've made some poor choices. Growing up, we messed up a time or two; perhaps we have some skeletons in our closets. As adults and as parents we have also failed and have frequently been misguided. We may have acted in haste and not been very loving. Yet knowing this, why is it so difficult to sincerely admit our mistakes to others, especially to our children? Perhaps we were taught that parents are to set good examples and that admitting mistakes would make a bad impression. We think we must be perfect, but inside we know we are not.

If we all were truly mature, we would instantly recognize when we've wounded someone else and quickly and freely apologize. To the extent we can do that, we model the behavior we want our children to adopt. But whether we admit it or not, children know when we have blown it; so when your child confronts you with your misbehavior, acknowledge that it is true. It is such a relief for a child when parents recognize their own fallibilities. You know how you feel when you say something and someone responds, "That's not true." You feel bad. Not surprisingly, your child feels just as bad when you say something like that. But when you say, "Yes, I was wrong," or "I'm glad you brought that up," you have opened the door to honest two-way communication.

When a child is hurt he sometimes reacts by withdrawing, pouting, becoming cranky, or lashing out. Pay attention to those times, and ask your child about it: "Did I do something that hurt you?" "Did I disappoint you? "Have I let you down?" If he is feeling hurt, do not brush it off or pooh-pooh it by saying, "That's nothing to be upset about."

When an apology is due, give it freely, then follow your apology with action. Some parents say "I'm sorry," but then don't change their behavior, rendering the apology meaningless. Sarah's mother embarrassed her frequently by commenting in front of friends about her messy room. Sarah asked her many times to stop. Although Sarah's mom was quick to apologize, a week later she would be doing the same thing.

A courageous parent follows an apology with sincere soul searching, to discover if a change in behavior is warranted. When you can admit your mistakes and ask forgiveness, your child will respect your humility. When you change your behavior, he will see your inner courage. No matter how small or large the injustice, when you admit it, you have taken the first step toward rebuilding the bridge between yourself and your child. When you've messed up, don't justify or backpeddle; don't hide or disguise. Admit it, apologize, change your behavior, laugh about it, and move on.

Touch Gently

Touch is an expression of your love that goes beyond words. Touch is your first communication with your baby, and throughout our life it remains our most vulnerable and tender connection with others.

Because every touch has a feeling that comes with it, it's wise for you to master the language of touch. A light soft touch expresses your warm feelings for your child. It says, "I like you." A warm and gentle hug conveys, "I'll take care of you." It's an affectionate embrace that says, "You're safe." Is your touch kind and tender? Do you give light strokes and reassuring pats? Or do you hit, yank, pull, push, poke, slap, squeeze, pinch, thump, or spank? Parents who resort to harsh touching to influence children seem to generate resentment and anger more than anything else. Sure, it may get the child's attention momentarily, but in the long run it builds walls of isolation. Children who are spanked, hit, or slapped learn very quickly to do the same. Deep down inside they know that beating up on someone else is wrong, but they can't stop themselves. They imitate their parents by resorting to physical brawn to express frustration. They'll think that if you are bigger and stronger you can get away with it because, after all, their parents get away with hitting them. I recommend a different approach.

42

Have you ever noticed when someone takes your hand or touches you with love and sensitivity that a wonderful phenomenon occurs? Stress and tension dissolve. Fear recedes. Babies fall asleep in such soothing arms. Children unwind and calm down with a gentle, reassuring touch. And a word to the wise: Experts agree that premature sexual experimentation stems from a hunger for loving touch. So hold and cuddle your child as much as you can. As he grows, give affectionate hugs when he's near. Hold hands if he will let you. But remember, never force a touch or a hug on a child; like all of us, he has a right to maintain a comfort zone around his own physical space.

At twelve, Craig didn't want his mom to hug him, but sometimes when she stood close by, he leaned into her. It was his way of touching without too much closeness. Tony told his grandpa, "Please don't hug me when you drive me to school." His grandpa respected his wishes and winked a good-bye instead. But when the child gives you the go-ahead, it's okay to reach out with tenderness so that your touch is a compassionate source of comfort now and always.

Teach That All Feelings Are Acceptable

※⅄※⅄※⅄

Feelings are part of being human; they bring sensitivity to life. Without feelings we would all be predictable robots on automatic pilot—boring, dull, lifeless. Children who've been allowed to express all their feelings, including the not-so-loving ones, have a big jump start toward believing in themselves and getting along with others. From the many shades of fear and anger to the subtle expressions of love and contentment, you and your child will experience a wide range and intensity of feelings. That's normal.

Accept all your child's feelings as natural and don't dwell on whether they make sense. Many times feelings come in contradictory pairs—eagerness and hesitation, happiness and sadness, love and hate. You can feel two or more feelings at the same time, so don't get hung up on one. This is what I mean: One day at around seven years old, Manda was mad at me for some reason and screamed, "I hate you, I hate you!" and ran to her room, yelling loudly and slamming her door. Later when I walked by, hanging on her door was a large note: "Dear Mom, I hate you more than anyone can! Love, Manda."

Never tell a child that what she is feeling is wrong. If you are uncomfortable with negative emotions, remember that when a negative feeling is expressed and not judged, it miraculously loses its destructive power; it is when such feelings are repressed and internalized that they do their damage. When a child's feelings are accepted, she will feel less lonely, angry, and fearful, more sure of herself, and not so compelled to behave so toughly and uncaringly.

When a child expresses any kind of feeling—from anger, to fear, to joy—she does not want judgment, logic, advice, or reassurance. In the midst of a strong emotional outburst, she does not want to explain or justify; she simply needs your understanding. A child wants you to comprehend whatever she is feeling, and when you do, it gives her great relief, knowing she can trust you with her feelings. Your acceptance of these feelings dispels them, so once again your child is calm.

Parents who cannot tolerate their child's feelings know the child only on the surface; they will never be close or know one another's hearts, and there will always be distance between them. But parents who accept the waves of contradictory feelings within themselves and their children foster depth and authenticity in their relationship.

Speak to Their True Feelings

❧❧❧

As a parent you have a big job in understanding what is going on inside your child and yourself; it's especially difficult if you were scolded, ridiculed, or shamed for your feelings as a child. If this happened, you probably became disconnected from your emotions in some way and now, as a parent, it is easy to be confused when your child expresses something you don't understand. But to raise a fully functioning person, you must be attuned to all of your child's feelings, including those he doesn't understand himself. You will often have to use your intuition to discover what is going on, because your child won't always say it with words. This is one of the most challenging aspects of parenting.

When a child is unreasonable, unmanageable, uncooperative, anxious, withdrawn, fussy, moody, or behaving in ways you don't understand, he is struggling with feelings he cannot express. It is your job to help him discover what they might be. When the Millers brought their new baby home, they thought they had prepared Erica for her sister's arrival. They took extra care to make sure Erica got plenty of special attention, so when she started throwing herself on the floor and crying for no apparent reason, they were baffled. As Linda was feeding the baby, Erica sat in the corner crying. Her mom's reassurance didn't help. Then Linda said to Erica, "Are you mad?" She handed Erica a doll and said, "Show me how mad you are—it's okay." Erica spanked the doll and wrung its neck. Linda did not chastise her, but said, "Come tell me the next time you're feeling so mad." After only a couple more crying jags, with her mother's gentle acceptance, Erica's jealousy was gone.

Parents tend to treat their children in ways *they* were treated growing up. As an adult Clarke was always angry and negative. He complained, poked fun, and ridiculed everyone, was never happy or upbeat, and had a quick temper. Even so, he was shocked when his son, Jason, threw things when something went wrong. Clarke punished Jason for being destructive and wondered why their family life was so tense.

Children are little mirrors that reflect our emotional life. If you don't understand what your child is feeling, tune in to your *own* feelings first. Step back and ask yourself, "What do I feel? What is going on inside me?" You might discover, as Clarke did, that all along *he* was the one who was upset and that Jason was reflecting that by acting out. When Clarke changed his behavior, so did Jason. By tuning in to your inner voice, you will be better able to respond to your child's true feelings.

Let Them Cry

Tears have many dimensions. There are tears of pain and suffering and tears of happiness and delight. There are the loud cries of a newborn signaling "I'm hungry" or "Hold me—I'm lonely." A mother learns quickly to understand the meaning of her baby's cry.

But it's not just babies that cry. As they grow, of course, there will be many times when both boys and girls need to cry. Tears are a natural way of mending a broken heart and letting go of disappointment. Tears can be an overflowing of happiness and a running over of a heart full of pure joy. Although it might be disturbing to see your child cry, sometimes it is the only release that will calm him.

Even if your child's tears make you feel helpless, please don't ever try to stop them; this will make him feel ashamed and teach him to repress his emotions. If you want to do something when your child is crying, ask quietly, "Can I put my arms around you?" If he is willing, gently hold him and tell him it's okay to cry. Let him know that tears are a sign of a sensitive, loving person. Don't judge or embarrass him. Let him cry until he has emptied himself of his pain and hurt before you ask what his tears were all about.

Don't force him to talk, because sometimes he just doesn't know for sure. Sometimes the tears themselves are the only expression needed. If you don't interfere, tears will bring relief and soon he'll feel energetic and happy once again.

When Jerry accidentally hit a baseball through the neighbors' front window, he ran into his house sobbing so deeply he couldn't catch his breath. No words of comfort would do—just his father holding him was the understanding he needed. When he was finally able to catch his breath, he told his story, and his dad started laughing. "Jerry, at the ballpark that would have been a home run!" And with that they walked next door for a talk. What a blessed relief for a child when a parent can be empathetic!

Don't Hide Your Tears

Just as you would not squelch their tears, never suppress your own. Crying comes with parenting, and tears will come in many ways. There are the tears of jubilance as you hold your newborn for the first time and tears of sorrow when realize that you have acted in haste or said something you didn't mean. There are tears of anguish when you see your children in pain and tears of relief when they come home safe.

Sometimes tears come when you least expect them. Something your child does or says will seem so innocent yet so profound that the tears slowly roll down your cheeks. For example, Marcus took his stepdaughter, Janey, to the father-daughter banquet. One by one each girl stood up, introduced her father, and said a few words. When it was Janey's turn she read an original essay that began, "What my stepdad has done for me . . . ." He could not believe his ears as his eight-year-old daughter read a list of the things he had taught her, some of which he had long forgotten. "The first thing I remember learning from my stepdad was how to tie my shoelaces. He was a patient teacher. He taught me to walk on a balance beam and do a handstand. My stepdad showed me how to use a hammer and paint my bedroom." The list went on and ended with, "now my stepdad is teaching me to drive his boat. I love you, Dad." Janey sat down and took his hand—and with that his tears overflowed.

Tears come with parenting. Don't worry so much *why* you are crying—that is not as important as simply allowing the release. Tears cleanse, they clear the dust, they clarify your vision. You will feel relieved after a good cry. Tears are a sign that your heart is open; you are alive and feeling the tugs to your heart—the warmth is there. It's nothing to be ashamed of or hide. If you allow your tears to flow freely, an amazing thing happens and soon you'll be laughing freely. Laughter and tears go together—sometimes you will laugh so hard you'll start to cry and sometimes you'll cry so hard you'll start to laugh.

Some parents have the misguided notion that it is harmful for a child to see you upset. That doesn't have to be true, so long as you don't hold the child responsible for making you feel better. One day when I was sitting on the edge of my bed having a good cry, Manda, six years old, sat down beside me and lovingly put her arms around my neck. As I put my head on her little shoulder, she said, "It's like I'm the mom and you're the kid." I nodded and she added, "It's okay to cry Mom, but do you mind if I close the door, 'cause you are really bothering me." With that she kissed my cheek and said, "Call me if you need me."

Make Room for the Crankies and the Quarrels

From time to time everyone in your household is going to be moody, out-of-sorts, temperamental, or just plain hard to live with. And every family has disagreements, little annoyances, and complaints with one another. But the crankies and the quarrels do not have to ruin your day or your family life. When you've had a bad day, there's no reason to take it out on yourself, your spouse, or your kids; and there's no need to be miserable just because your spouse is being difficult or your child is being fussy.

Adam and Theresa wanted everyone to get along and be happy. They were opposed to family conflicts, and negative feelings were not allowed to surface. They never fought and they expected the kids to do as they were told. If the children talked back or fought with one another, they were grounded. This seemed to work until one of the sons started using drugs. Eventually they went to family counseling, where they uncovered many unresolved conflicts and plenty of upsets. Although their family life is at times unpleasant, they now know it's better to face problems as they arise rather than put a lid on them and leave them to simmer.

They started using the steps to win-win conflict resolution: First, schedule a meeting for airing concerns. Second, allow everyone to voice complaints without name calling, blaming, interrupting, or questioning. The third phase is a brainstorm session for possible solutions, and the fourth is the thinking time. Everyone thinks about the possible solutions and what they would be willing to do. The fifth step is to choose a solution everyone can live with, making compromises if necessary. Sixth, put the solution into action and work out the kinks at the next meeting.

It's a good idea to teach your children how to voice their complaints and how to respond to yours. Let them know that they can disagree with you and that you won't put them down for it. Demonstrate how you can arrive at creative solutions together.

When dealing with family crankies and quarrels remember you can't always please your children. If you try to, you will lose yourself. Likewise they will not always please you, so don't make them feel as though they have to. You don't have to be right all the time and, when you are right, it isn't always necessary to make it known. Don't exacerbate the problem by turning it into an issue of who's right or wrong. Choose your battles carefully. If you make a big deal out of everything, the important things get lost in the shuffle. Overlook the small stuff and remind yourself that healthy quarrels with win-win resolutions can lead to better communication and a more cooperative family life. And just because one person is cranky, not everyone has to get flustered.

Teach Values by Example

❦❦❦

Children learn their values from watching you. Values are not taught directly but rather assimilated and absorbed, and by this subtle process of identification your children will imitate you. For example, if you value polite manners but speak to your children rudely, they will never get the hang of it. If you value gentleness, be gentle with your children. They take note of what you do more than of what you say. The old cliché, "Do as I say, not as I do" is not only ineffective, it sends mixed messages that are both confusing and unfair to a child.

The Daltons put great emphasis on money. They talked about their bank accounts over breakfast and watched the stock market closely. They were cautious spending money, but whatever they bought was always the best. When dining with friends they were meticulous in dividing the bill. They talked about the prices of things and were proud of saving money. They charged their kids rent and lectured about the cost of living. They were puzzled because their kids couldn't keep jobs and were always wanting to borrow money. The twenty year old refused to work for minimum wage, even though he bought a fancy jeep. "Money is important to us," they asked, "so why isn't it important to them?" On the surface that seemed true, but looking closely it was clear that the kids were *exactly* like their parents. They too thought in terms of money—how much we get, how we can keep it for ourselves, and what we can buy. The Daltons had wanted to teach the value of financial management, but what they had conveyed instead was the love of money.

Teaching values is a very delicate undertaking. What values do you want to impart to your children? Do you practice what you preach? Do you value honesty but when they tell the truth, do you in some way punish them? Rose asked Jena, her four year old, "Did you color on the walls?"

"No," she answered, scared to death.

"You'd better tell the truth," Rose warned. When Jena confessed, her mother took the crayons away, gave her a spanking, and lectured her for lying. What did Jena learn? That telling the truth hurts.

Remember that you are teaching by your example in your daily life. Practice emotional honesty by embodying the values you want to instill in your children. If your home is a peaceful, nurturing, safe place to grow up, you are doing your part.

Honor Their Differences

No two kids are alike. By the second month of a baby's life, he or she is already displaying a unique personality. Some babies smile and laugh freely, others are more serious and subdued. There are calm, quiet babies and babies whose arms and legs are constantly moving. Some babies sleep a lot, others stay awake. Some babies have tempers, some are sociable, some are sensitive to strangers, some are little performers who like lots of attention. Some babies entertain themselves, others are high maintenance.

Just as there are differences in looks and temperament, there are variations in learning styles, talents, interests, and abilities. Some kids are naturally math whizzes whereas others excel in drawing. Some love to compete in team sports while others prefer to read alone in a treehouse. Some children get lost in computer games; others want lots of friends around and talk on the phone for hours. Some kids are pleasant and cooperative, others fight for their point of view every time. And although this makes life more complicated, it also keeps it lively. Vive la différence.

Since everyone is different there is no need to make comparisons. If you notice a tendency to compare yourself to others, you will have the same tendency to compare your child to other children, or your children to each other. Comparison is a kind of disease: it breeds contention—and not the healthy kind of sporting competition, but a deep-rooted sense of inadequacy, of an inability to measure up. In this kind of competition one must be *better* in order to simply be okay.

Some parents start comparing from the very beginning, but the practice is pointless. There will always be some child somewhere who is smarter or kinder or more talented than your own. In such a scrutinizing and discriminating environment, a child does not have a fair chance to develop as a unique and special individual.

All children grow and learn at their own natural pace, and comparison has no part whatsoever. Remember, a baby doesn't learn to walk by being compared with other babies; rather, in a sense, he learns to walk when praised for doing a lousy job of walking. When he stands up by the couch, takes two steps, and falls down, Dad and Mom drop whatever they're doing, proclaim, "Johnny's walking!" and applaud him with enthusiasm. They even write it in the baby book. But can you imagine what would happen if they said, "It's about time . . . His *sister* was *running* by his age." Johnny might never try again!

Throw out the imaginary yardstick. Your pleasure will mount as these unique and special beings blossom in the light of your unconditional love.

Share Your Dreams

❧ ❧ ❧

Everybody dreams. We dream when we sleep, and everyone has daydreams, wishes, and secret longings as well—children too. Everybody thinks about tomorrow. Like you, children imagine how their life will be. Planning and wishing, visualizing and dreaming are the first steps toward becoming who we want to be. Dreams and wishes long to be shared, and dreams shared out loud take on new dimensions. Sharing your dreams unlocks the door to self-discovery.

Five-year-old Wendy told me, "I had the scariest dream."

"Oh?" I said. "Draw me a picture."

"I can't," she sighed.

"Would you like to try?" She took the paper and crayons and drew the most magnificent multicolored animals. "So colorful!" I said.

"Yes, yes, I'm a very good drawer. Can I hang them on your wall?" she asked, and quickly added, "They won't scare us now 'cause I made them happy." She had transformed a frightening dream into a happy picture. The dream images unfolded on their own, and we didn't force a thing.

When sharing a nighttime dream, it isn't important what the dream might mean. When sharing a daydream, it doesn't matter if it will come true. What is far more valuable is placing the emphasis on the sharing, the unfolding, the learning, and the mutual insight that comes. Share your dreams as a way of knowing each other better.

Making dream maps works well for this. A dream map is a poster with pictures and words that represent what you are wishing for. Cut out pictures and words from magazines that symbolize what you want for yourself. Make a collage on posterboard, hang your dream maps where you can see them daily, and watch what happens.

At twelve, Jody told me she was depressed and had nothing to look forward to. She had no goals and nothing excited her anymore. I suggested she make a dream map and bring it to the office to share. Three weeks later she brought it in and told me about each picture. She surprised herself with what she discovered and started riding her bicycle soon after, just as she had pasted on her map.

Everything starts with an idea, a dream, a vision, and when shared and encouraged, your children's dreams and aspirations can become a reality. One night you might wake up, as Anthony's parents did, to find your child sitting on your bed, telling you of plans to be an actor. Anthony tried out for a part in a theater production and got the supporting role. Share your dreams—they will help you discover yourself and each other in new and wondrous ways.

Expressions

*While laughing with your child
you'll take a peek at heaven.*

Change Your Routine

✿✿✿

Children are naturally curious about everything. They want to know it, see it, feel it, taste it, and explore it fully. They come into the world without set ideas, and from the beginning they want to learn it all. By the age of three, they are walking, talking, little question machines. "Why are the clouds fluffy?" "Where does the rain go?" "Why is Grandma old?" "Why? why? why?" By accepting their curiosity, you not only give them permission to learn, you make learning a lifetime adventure, for the way you welcome their inquisitiveness will influence their attitude toward school and their own intelligence. Sadly, when children's curiosity is not supported and encouraged, they shut down and learning becomes more difficult.

One way to keep them exploring is to expand your world and live creatively yourself. Infants need routine, but as they grow they will want change too. It's usually easier to stick to an established routine, but when you try something out of the ordinary you find new vitality and a spurt of mental energy. Everyone needs a change once in a while—you do, and so does your child.

When you feel stuck in a rut, bored, or anxious, it's time to change your routine. Surprise your child by taking her out to lunch on a school day. Be a little daring: Go to the movies on a school night and let him sleep late. You'll be amazed at what little changes will do for your imagination. Eat dinner picnic-style or have a campout in the backyard, swap chores, play a board game making up new rules, or plan a child's night out. Little switches in routine that don't take much time can add new dimensions to family life.

Talk it over, take a chance, try a new approach; you'll teach your child that there are lots of options and many ways to do things. An atmosphere rich in firsthand experiences is the best way for a child to learn.

Laugh, Dance, and Sing Together

※ ※ ※

A nurturing home is a place where parents and children can relax and unwind from the pressures of the day. Laughing, singing, and dancing are the fastest ways to transform worries into celebration. Having fun together will strengthen your family and foster easy, honest relationships among all of you. And as your children grow they are much more likely to enjoy being with the family if everyone is having a good time.

A home filled with music is an exciting place to be. Begin when the children are young by sharing lullabies from your childhood. Create personalized versions of favorite tunes. Encourage your children to teach you songs they've learned, and let them check out tapes from the library. Play music when you're doing the dishes; do a little jig when you're shaking up the orange juice. Your kids will get a kick out of it and you'll contribute to a pleasant home life that includes good-natured fun; but, more important, you're creating an atmosphere where family members can be easygoing with each other, which is critical to open communication, especially with teens.

Ed and Clarice practiced the tango in the family room as their two boys rolled on the floor laughing hysterically. They had so much fun they did it over and over. And while sharing these moments of laughter with their children, they just about mastered the tango.

Bill's kids can tell when he's home, because the stereo is cracking. He listens to everything—Mozart, Bach, the Beatles, Elton John. Although the kids tease him about his taste in music, they like it too, but for a different reason—it's comforting to know that Dad is enjoying himself.

Introduce your children to all kinds of music; there's nothing like it for pleasure and relaxation, and it is so easily shared. Some studies indicate that babies respond to soothing music even before they're born. One mother I know loved to dance and piped music throughout the house. She told her children, "Music is nourishment for your soul." Although she never forced them, they all were exposed to her passion at an early age; and it probably won't surprise you to know that each child easily learned to play musical instruments. When traveling in the car, singing helps pass the time. On errands around town, Lynne makes sure she has a wide variety of music tapes to keep the kids entertained.

Laughter serves as a bridge between you and your child, bringing you closer. Laugh often; tell little jokes without poking fun or teasing. Look at the humorous side of life. When laughter and music are common threads running through your encounters with your child, family life is more exciting, and precious memories are made. Have a song in your heart. Be free with your laughter, spontaneous with your dance, and your children will think of you with a twinkle in their eye.

Call Them Love Names

Love names are those little monikers that make your heart melt. Using pet names like skookums, sweetie-pie, honey bunch, smoochie-girl, lovey, or pookey-poo is like sharing a special, heartfelt secret. Love names tell your child that you enjoy her company—that she is extra special and this is the name you use for only her. It is a simple, lighthearted way of reaching out to bring your children close, to tell them they are precious and valuable. While driving in the car, Jane and her stepchildren were quite creative in coming up with different names for each other: "Jokey Jane," "Silly Willy," "Sunshine Shelly." Everyone was involved, laughing at the funny sounds and meanings; ten years later the whole family fondly remembers this name game.

Love names tell your children they have a corner of your heart forever. I made up a song for Amanda using her love name, "Amanda, Manda, Panda Poo." I write her love names on the cards I give her, and I knew she liked them when she started signing her own notes and cards this way. She has also given me several love names, and when she uses one like "Momma-lu," I feel great. We gave her aunt, a cousin, and friends special love names too.

66

Love names are reassuring and fun. Remember, however, that because love names are terms of endearment they are best used in private. Never use the name to embarrass or ridicule your child, and it is probably best not to use love names in front of their friends, unless you have checked it out with them beforehand and they truly don't mind.

If you have ever been called a love name by a parent or grandparent, you know how heartwarming that can be. Isn't it amazing that no matter how old you are, upon hearing your love name warm shivers run through you and suddenly you feel cared for? If you haven't already, bestow on your child a special love name now for a lifetime full of gladness.

Send Them Love Letters

Love letters are personalized little notes to your kids that let them know you're fondly thinking of them. They are little messages of sunshine to brighten up their day. They are surprises that pop up when and where your child least expects. Put little notes under pillows, paste them on bathroom mirrors, or, for noontime pick-me-ups, stash one in their lunch boxes. Amber's dad packed her lunch daily and always included a note. She looked forward to finding them even as she got older. Sometimes he sent a joke, an inspiring word, an interesting fact, a piece of gossip, a cartoon, or a brief hello with a happy face. When she went away to college, more than his lunches, she missed his notes.

Tuck one in a pocket or a shoe for a unexpected thrill. Drop them in drawers or pin them inside of jackets. Consider sending one through the mail—receiving one's first letter delivered by the mailman can bring so much excitement to a child that it's well worth the cost of a stamp. I know a father whose thirteen-year-old daughter was coping with a bitter disappointment, so he sent a special letter delivered to her school. This extra effort lifted her spirits and gave her courage, while proving beyond a doubt that even teenagers benefit from special attention from often-dismissed parents.

Get in the habit of note writing when they are young. Allyson taught her twins to read with big notes pasted all over the house. As they get older note writing can come in very handy for solving disagreements or conflicts by avoiding lengthy discussions. Kids of all ages frequently respond better to a note reminding them to get a chore done, than to mom's voice nagging them once again. One mom taped reminder notes to the bathroom mirror, where they couldn't go unnoticed: "Please empty the dishwasher by 4 P.M. today so we have clean dishes for supper." Her daughter completed the job and left a response for Mom: "Thanks, but I'd rather have food." The task was done and they enjoyed a good chuckle.

Sending notes is another way of letting your children know how important they are. When Zack went off to summer camp, his parents wrote him a letter sharing special memories from their own camp experiences and offering him good-natured, practical advice: "Call home on Sunday night," "Take at least one shower," and "Change your underwear." This let him know that in his absence they were thinking of him. Letters written from your heart will perk up your child's day. Write that you love them and thank them for what they have taught you and for the chores that they do.

Build Lots of Blanket Forts

Have you noticed that little children like to play and sleep in cozy places? It seems to be a natural instinct that little folks have. Forts in the house and tents in the backyard bring delight to every child. Some of my fondest memories are of my mother taking the cushions off the couch and letting us use blankets to design our hideaways.

When Manda was five she loved to sleep in her closet. One day I saw her walk past me with a hammer and nails and heard pounding. "What are you doing?"

"Building a tent," she answered. I went to look and, sure enough, she was nailing her designer sheets and comforter to the walls of her closet. Oh, well, I thought, what good are sheets if not to be enjoyed and, besides, she was having so much fun. She slept in there for about six weeks. Then she hung blankets from the staircase to construct a new hiding place. These colorful forts *did* mess up our house, but seeing the sparkle in her eyes quickly turned any inconvenience into pure joy. At seven and a half she went through a neat phase and spent hours cleaning her room and rearranging her drawers. Your kids probably will too.

Forts provided hours of entertainment for the kids in our neighborhood as well. Ruth Ann let the kids build forts in the basement. Kevin built a ship in the bathtub, complete with rugs so he wouldn't slip. A fort is fun, be it a treehouse or a cardboard box; imagination unfolds and children spend hours creating an exciting new world. It's possible that imaginary playmates might join in the fun.

Nothing can turn a rainy day into an adventure, or a bored and cranky child into a creative genius, like a blanket fort in the dining room; and eating lunch or spending the night in one is pure luxury. In the summer, tents in the backyard or on the deck are great for sleepovers. Try it, you'll see what I mean.

Fly Kites Together

❧❧❧

It has been said that play is valuable work for children, and if you have ever watched a three-month-old baby intently involved with hand play, you understand why. The baby examines his hands closely, noticing patterns, colors, shapes, and sounds. Play is meaningful, creative, and a vital component of a child's development. Through play children develop social skills, interact with playmates, resolve conflicts, and express their thoughts and feelings, gain knowledge, and use their imaginations. They will do this alone, with siblings, friends, strangers, and with you. From peek-a-boo to marbles to hopscotch, playing with your children will lighten your day.

Enjoying spontaneous, uninhibited play is a natural and refreshing expression of your vitality. When you allow your adult worries and responsibilities to subside for a while, a miracle of togetherness happens and lasting memories are made. Playing with your children does not have to be expensive nor a day-long affair. No fancy toys are needed, nor elaborate plans. Deborah taught her kids to juggle using marshmallows; Tony looks forward to the summer months when he can play scotch, an updated version of hide-n-seek, with his kids and the neighbors. A lighthearted pillow fight while you change the beds, or a quick game of tag in the backyard—

spontaneous, fun for everyone, and good exercise too!

Jack grew up in a poor family in a small beach town. Even with little money, he never felt deprived because his family always found ways to play. Flying handmade kites together on the beach was one way. Each year he and his sister and five brothers, along with their parents, would participate in the annual kite festival. They'd spend months designing and constructing their kites, and hours practicing trick flying. The trophies and ribbons they won were displayed in a glass case. The recognition was nice, they were thrilled when they won, but what Jack remembers most was just being together. Now, as a father, Jack makes sure that playing with his children is part of every week—he's even bought his eleven month old a kite.

Flying kites together makes you feel free and joyous. As the wind takes hold of the kite, you can feel it on your body, gently rocking you back and forth. The sky quietly accepts you, surrounding you and protecting you. You become a child yourself and your spirit is set free. When you disappear with the clouds, the dividing line between you and your child dissolves. Look at the clouds and share the stories they tell. Run with the wind, or roll on the ground. There are no rules, just freedom. You can't force a kite; you just have to accept where the winds take it. A wonderful metaphor for life.

Lighten Up

❧❧❧

Parenting is important—probably the most important role in your life—but you don't need to approach it so strictly and seriously all the time. Parenting can be fun if you lighten up. It makes family life more stimulating and relaxed, and children are more cooperative and learn more easily in a lighthearted atmosphere. Problems are more easily solved and worries are better kept in perspective. Children thrive on the tender loving care of a happy parent. Life is so short. Don't freak out over how they dress; it really is not a crime to wear mix-match. And don't get so uptight if they want to skip a bath—they won't get ill.

Your children are with you for such a short time. Take every opportunity to be happy so that you can savor the moments. To be serious, burdened, constantly critical and negative requires so much effort. But to be relaxed and lighthearted comes much more naturally and is healthier too. Your children will be much more manageable when you're not stressed out. Slow down. It requires a shift in focus from the demanding task at hand, and you may have to remind yourself about what your priorities really are, but your whole family will benefit. The dishes may sit in the sink a little longer, or that load of laundry may go undone for another day, but were they *really* more important than sharing a bedtime story with your preschooler and talking about her day?

Even in a crisis the lighthearted approach will always get things moving on the right track more easily. Stephanie, nine years old, was screaming at her mother, "You are *so* mean!" When her dad walked into the room, he could tell by the tension in the air that a big fight was brewing. "What's wrong?" he asked.

"Oh, Mom is *soooo* . . . mean!"

He listen closely as Stephanie told the whole story, and then advised, "Well, just consider her your very own personal meanie." With that, they all laughed.

When you find yourself overloaded with responsibilities and ready to scream because the trash can is overflowing, the checkbook is unbalanced, the dog is unfed, and no one is helping out, stop for a moment and ask yourself, "Will this matter tomorrow, next week, next year?" Chances are it won't, but what *will* matter is the quality of your relationship with your family. No one will care that the floor needed mopping, but someone very well may remember being yelled at by a frazzled mom. Seriousness and unhappiness are habits that you can change with a shift in perspective. When your toddler "helps" you with the dishes, look at her beaming face rather than the puddles on the floor. Remember your priorities. You can do your daily routine with a grudge and a groan or with a cheerful spirit. The choice is yours.

Take Time Away

Nobody wants to be together all the time. Children need time away from you and you need time away from them. Whether it is a little break in the day or a weekend getaway, being apart can refresh everyone.

Start with a little getaway when they are babies. Allie sits on the front steps and reads while her three month old naps. Sometimes she hires a sitter so she can ride her bike. Although it is true that some babies adapt well to a loving caretaker and others rebel, as long as you find a trustworthy sitter a little time away won't hurt and can do you worlds of good. Martha feels a twinge as she leaves her one year old, Andrew, while she takes a pottery class. He always cries as she walks out the door, but each time she comes back she finds him playing happily.

Time away can add new insights to your life and will help you appreciate each other more. When they reach school age your kids will start wanting to spend the night with friends. Juan, six years old, started spending Friday nights with his buddy. His dad, a single parent, missed him but decided it was good for Juan to find out how other families live, so he didn't take it personally; he found that he enjoyed his time alone.

Don't make excuses that you are too busy. Todd convinced Meryl to join him on a weekend business trip when their twins were just two. Meryl was in agony for the first six hours or so, but when she called home and found that her mother had everything under control, she relaxed. Now they go away each fall, leaving their four teenagers to care for themselves. They call it their "necessary for sanity trip."

You need regular time to be alone, to reflect, to sit quietly. You also need time to talk privately with your spouse or friends. For a short break, go to the bedroom for a nap or soak in the tub. A fifteen-minute time-out can revitalize you and your child. Lisa told her five and seven year olds: "I'm feeling cranky, so I'm taking a time-out in my getaway chair." It worked.

Take a weekend outing alone. If you feel a little guilty, remember that a little guilt is preferable to pile of resentments because you never have time for yourself. When you are stressed-out, burned-out, or suffering from too much togetherness, the best way to deal with it is to announce honestly to your child, "It's time for my break. I need a half hour alone." Then hang out the "Do not disturb" sign. In fact, make sure each family member has a "Do not disturb" sign to hang on their door when they need to get away and be alone.

Read Books Aloud

Books educate, entertain, and stimulate the imagination. Reading books out loud will put a new spin on togetherness. When my daughter was small, she had so much energy she was awake and wide-eyed late at night while I was sometimes exhausted. So every night I would read aloud to her, hoping she would fall asleep. She always loved it and I read one every night. Frequently I dozed off in the middle of a story. But even when I didn't, she never wanted me to stop reading. That's when I put the advantages of modern technology to work. I started recording our reading sessions on tape. Then she could listen to the story tape whenever she wanted. They provided comfort when I was away. Our friend, Ashoka, did the same. He taught her a little French, German, and Italian this way. Sometimes he would read the story in English and add a little French for flavor. We even made her tapes together, reading all kinds of stories: fairy tales, rhymes, adventures, and the classics. We added music. She could then play them any time of the day or night. She took her Walkman, earphones, and tapes on car trips and other occasions when she thought she might be bored. She is now sixteen, an avid reader, and occasionally still listens to the tapes we made.

A great gift idea is to buy a book, record it on tape, and then give both. The whole family can make a tape together, each taking turns reading parts of the story, playing the part of one or more characters, or reading with a funny voice. Tapes make a much better baby-sitter than the television. Certainly turning off the television and reading books is better for the nerves, not to mention the mind. You can do this for your child or with your child; make one for the grandparents—it's a personalized gift to last a lifetime.

Create a Circle of Quiet

Have you ever noticed that children can get so wound up they can't calm down? Get cranky, demanding, and whiny with too much stimulation? Like adults, children need quiet time each day. We sometimes get so focused on activities for our children that we forget to teach them about quiet time. It's well worth the effort to help your family discover the pleasure of silence and the advantages of slowing down and taking life a little more easily.

Circles of quiet are soothing to the nervous system; silence is the best tranquilizer. Creating a circle of quiet helps children unwind and relax. A fussy baby will calm down much more quickly when held by a parent who is relaxed, inwardly centered, and still. A parent whose nerves are frazzled and whose energy is chaotic transmits that to the baby. Margo, a mother of a newborn, did yoga to quiet herself while her husband took the baby in a stroller and went for a run.

It is through these circles of quiet that your child will discover the difference between the outer world and his own inner world. Through silence your child will come to know himself and learn about his inner life.

When studying for the bar exam, Daniel needed more quiet in the evenings, so he taught his twin boys the "Shh and silence game." He made buttons that said, "*Shh,* I'm in silence." The boys learned that when dad was wearing his button, it was time for quiet play or reading. They came to respect their dad's need for study time, and learned to entertain themselves and become self-sufficient, and now they know what to do on a rainy day. They're not afraid of being alone with themselves.

Some families are so busy with an overbooked schedule of activities and responsibilities that they never take time to unwind, sit down, and be still. Some parents talk so much that the kids just tune out. Other families are so addicted to television and background noise they have to have something blaring all the time, regardless of whether anyone is listening.

Children who are able to simply play alone in a quiet space learn to understand their need for solitude. From a young age Max would say to his parents, "I like quiet." Circles of quiet in your home are the beginning of self-awareness and meditation. During quiet times a child feels tranquil and serene. Creating circles of quiet in your home from the very beginning will help you and your children find inner peace.

Play Hooky Together

Do you remember when you were a kid and pretended to have a stomachache or the flu? You weren't really sick, but you needed the day off. So you stayed in bed moaning and groaning, hoping your mom would show you mercy by not insisting you go to school. You felt guilty, but desperately needed a mental-health day. Sometimes your mom would give you a break, other times she'd call your bluff.

If you want to avoid such unnecessary hassles with your kids, why not play hooky together? Surely you too could use a break once in a while. If it makes you feel better, remember, one of the ways a child feels loved is when you take time from your busy schedule to give him your undivided attention.

At least twice each winter on a sunny day, the McAllisters call the school to say, "The kids won't be in today; our family has to go skiing." A change of pace adds spice to life. One day of hooky can give you new spurts of enthusiasm to carry on with the daily routine.

I let Manda play hooky occasionally and I don't think it has hurt her one bit; in fact, it has been an important part of her education. Sometimes she would stay in bed and read for the entire day. Another time she stayed home to clean and rearrange her room. I joined her by doing the same. Sometimes we would go on a special outing, visit the museum, and have lunch. Once she spent half the day accompanying me on work errands.

Sometimes the idea to play hooky was hers and other times it was mine. We seldom planned it in advance—it just seemed to arise at the right moment when one or the other of us needed it most. Manda never took advantage of this special treat; I think just knowing she had the choice was enough. Now that she is in high school, she tells me she is too busy to play hooky with me, but I keep hoping she'll find the time soon!

Walk in the Rain

Rain is a good reminder of how our attitude can affect everything. Some folks let it destroy their day; others consider it a blessing.

Children seem to like the rain. They like to get wet and slosh around in puddles. One evening five-year-old Manda sat watching a rainstorm from the kitchen window. She was very excited and said, "Mom, I want to go outside and dance with the wind."

I cautioned her, "But you'll get wet."

"It's okay," she reassured me, "I'm dirty."

Laughing to myself, I let her go. She whirled and twirled, her arms outstretched. She stomped and laughed with glee, getting drenched to the skin. I decided, What the heck? and joined her for the outdoor shower. In that moment life felt fresh and simple. It was pure joy. We ended the evening wrapped in warm blankets, sipping hot chocolate together. It was much more fun than being so practical. She remembers that night to this day, and gave me a wonderful compliment: "You're crazy Mom, but it's a good crazy."

When it comes to enjoying the simple pleasures of life, children are our best teachers. Adults forget quickly and get caught up in the stupid little things that don't matter very much. So what if your shoes get wet when walking in the rain? By worrying about it you miss the fun of the moment. Kids can remind us to keep our attitude positive and our thoughts focused on what really makes our hearts sing.

On another stormy night the lights went out, and Manda and the neighborhood kids eagerly gathered in front of our fireplace to roast hot dogs and tell ghost stories by candlelight. I was a little perturbed by this inconvenience, as I had planned to get my housework done, but as I put on a sweater and another pair of socks, I could hear the kids laughing, and an inner voice reminded me that the dusting and vacuuming would still be there tomorrow, but not this moment. The kids piled in sleeping bags and roasted hot dogs and marshmallows, and I learned to avoid the tendency to be so parental! I learned to relax and let the rain fall.

Go Barefoot

❧❧❧

Have you ever noticed that little children love to pull off their shoes and socks whenever they can? Perhaps there are good reasons for this. Take off your shoes, take off your socks, and wriggle and wiggle your toes. Walk in the sand, walk on the grass, and feel the earth beneath your feet.

When you find that you are bringing work home from the office more frequently and perhaps neglecting the people you love; when you insist that chores be completed before you unwind and are taking the fun out of living; if you have a tendency to worry, become overwhelmed with responsibilities, or get stressed-out you might benefit from a barefoot adventure. Ask yourself: "Does work come before spending time with my children every time?" Instead of working so much, why not take off your shoes, paint your toenails red, or get a foot massage?

Kelly started taking off her shoes and clothes when she was nine months old. Her mother told me, "She refuses to wear anything scratchy or tight." Sure makes sense to me. If your clothes are comfy, you'll feel better, you'll think a little less, and move a whole lot more. With your shoes off you won't see the world in quite the same way.

Sam and Margaret have their kids take off their shoes inside the house.

Margaret says, "That way I don't have to worry and yell about mud on the floor or carpet." Sam agrees, "The house is so much quieter when the kids run around with their shoes off." In fact, they liked it so well, they began asking guests of all ages to do the same. This practice is becoming so commonplace that just seeing a pair of shoes by the front door will prompt guests to take off theirs first thing.

Being kind to your feet can relax you and enable you to be kinder to your children; after all, they're the only ones you've got! Take off tight shoes, wiggle those toes, and breathe. Let your feet remind you that your children need your time and a relaxed, more comfortable you!

Frame Their Art and Hang It on the Wall

❦ ❦ ❦

Have you ever noticed that all young children are artists? Creative geniuses ready to bloom and be discovered. Children can teach us so much about creativity—just watch them when they paint a picture. They become completely absorbed in the drawing and put their complete attention, concentration, and love into that one picture. They don't worry about what others think—they give it their all.

Creativity takes many forms. A four-year-old boy I know can take a watch apart and put it back together almost exactly the way it was. When his father discovered this curiosity, he recognized his son's mechanical ability. He buys old watches and clocks at garage sales; the little boy loves them better than toys.

Robin created a family art gallery by hanging string along one wall and securing the drawings and paintings with clothespins. She and the kids regularly contribute to that gallery. Paul framed and hung on his office wall the family portraits drawn by his four year old.

With art children learn to solve problems. When your child is angry, frustrated, or scared, drawing a picture and telling a story can help him work it through. When Riley was scheduled for surgery, his mother helped him draw pictures of what was ahead. Through art a child learns that there are many ways to look at things. A good reminder for parents, too. Never tell a child how to paint a picture. Who says a cow can't be red, and why must we color within the lines?

Always encourage creativity, for you never know where it might lead. A top Seattle department store carries jewelry designed with the drawings of a twelve-year-old girl. One mother used her son's pictures to make greeting cards; he now works on movies. A father designed his business cards using a logo that his daughter had scribbled on paper. It gave her quite a boost— today she is a graphic designer. Using the pictures her toddlers draw throughout the year, Janis makes calendars to send to the grandparents.

When a child explores her creativity she discovers her potential. When her potential is recognized and acknowledged, her future is secured. Frame their art and suddenly it looks suitable for any gallery. Hang it on the walls and they're ready to fly.

Stay Up Late Together

❧❧❧

When children are small, it's a good idea to establish a regular bed-time routine. But once in a while, it can be a great change of pace to stay up a little later, particularly as kids get older. The world looks different at night, and children want to see what's going on; they don't want to miss out. Perhaps they're simply not tired—some kids have too much energy to always go to bed as scheduled. This can be a problem for parents who are eager for the kids to get to bed so that they can have some time alone. But forcing kids to go to bed when they're not tired soon backfires with endless requests for drinks of water and trips to the bathroom.

If bedtime is becoming a hassle, perhaps you might want to try a new approach. Consider letting them stay up a little later and see what happens. Some parents avoid the battle-of-bedtime blues by saying, "So long as you don't disturb us, you can stay up, but we're going to bed." Seven-year-old Meg lasted until 11:05 P.M. once and was back in bed at her regular time the next night. Jim and Patty avoid bedtime tears by letting their three and four year olds sleep on the floor in sleeping bags. Now, instead of resisting going to bed, they look forward to "camping out."

Try a slumber party with your children. Let them invite a friend over, make a bed in the closet, sleep under their beds, or read stories quietly in the hall. Elizabeth bought a nightlight for three-year-old Clementine to read books by on those nights when she wasn't quite ready to go to sleep at bedtime. You'll be surprised at how such a simple compromise can turn bedtime drudgery into a pleasant change of pace.

By staying up later children begin to understand their natural sleep rhythms and discover how to unwind. They will fall asleep when they are sleepy and will begin to establish their own bedtimes. When they know they can have some control, bedtime struggles decrease. Of course, as teen-agers they will probably always be up later than you. Don't worry, that's natural too.

Delight in Silliness

Can you be a silly-willy or are you too far gone? If you can't act a little goofy once in a while, it might just be that you've grown so parental you've become disconnected from your mischievous, playful side. It could mean that you've forgotten about having fun in life. Are you more than likely to be slightly cranky? Or, worse yet, are you on the verge of becoming terribly bored and boring? Are you a workaholic?

Do your children often see you laugh? Sadly some parents squelch their children with too much seriousness, mistakenly equating teaching responsibility with always being stern and hardworking. Perhaps they don't know that silliness is a natural way of burning off excess energy after learning a new task or feeling a strong emotion. If you find yourself giving lectures about the good old days, you're stuck in a rut. It's probably time to take a leap forward, let your hair down, and see another point of view.

Perhaps you've been feeling a little weary and have started noticing the frown lines across your brow? If this is the case, you might need the therapy that only a child can deliver: jump on a trampoline and read Dr. Seuss out loud for starters. Ask yourself, "When was the last time I goofed off?" "When was I slightly foolish?" Yesterday, last week, last year? It's never too late! If you find yourself full of negativity and worry that nothing is going your way, stop to play a silly game with your child for just a half hour. Try Simon Says, or follow-the-leader, or a game of Crazy Eights. If doing it for yourself is not compelling enough, do it for her—let her see the child in you for a change; she'll be delighted.

Add silliness to your breakfast with cinnamon toast, hippopotamus pancakes, and orange juice tea through a straw. At noontime slurp root-beer floats and gobble heart-shaped mashed banana sandwiches. For your silly dinner try veggies and fingers dipped in peanut-butter sauce and sip hot chocolate soup. Silliness is healthy, too.

If you've become a stodgy old crank, ask a child to teach you to play. When feeling uptight, worried, or in a stew, pause for a silly moment; think silly, act silly, walk silly, talk silly. If you're hopelessly out of practice, look to your child for a cue; you won't find a more willing coach. Your child's laughter is the best remedy for what ails you.

Splash a Lot

Have you ever noticed that children, as well as adults, are fascinated by water? Everyone seems to gravitate toward it. From bathtubs to wading pools to the kitchen sink, children like touching and feeling it; they like to sprinkle and spray it. Water has magical healing powers—you feel better around it. It washes the blues away.

I remember when Manda showed me a scientific fact. She said, "Mommy, I like water—it jiggles." She wanted me to watch closely as she demonstrated her discovery. Slowly she poured the water into a glass and proudly pointed out that the water was round. Next she poured it into a square container and showed me that the water turned square. I must admit I was enthralled by her genius, as I had never thought of water in quite that way.

Let your kids be around water. Take them to a pool, a lake, a river, or the ocean and notice how life flows so easily.

Swimming is a family activity that's fun as well as great exercise. Visit your neighborhood pool when you're bored, tired, or cranky. In the summer have a squirt-gun water fight. Get a slippery slide or cool off in a sprinkler. Put your toes in a lake or get on a tube and float down a river.

Splash, even if it's just in the tub. When the temperature is high or you're just plain mad at the world, splashing cools you down inside and out.

Although knowing how to swim is important if your children are around bodies of water, don't turn water into a task to be mastered. One little boy told me he worried that he couldn't swim. Perhaps that was because his parents forced him to take lessons before he was ready. It was a battle every time. He would cry and they would threaten. They wasted a summer of swimming lessons on this tug-of-war. The very next year he jumped in willingly at the first lesson. It is much better to let children discover swimming at their own pace—there's no need to push. Never force children to go swimming. Just present them with the opportunity and they'll get the hang of it when they're ready.

Kids know instinctively what we have forgotten: that water can and should be fun, and that the joy of splashing is as important to them as the skill of swimming.

Giggle

Children are the merriment makers. With their miniature bodies they giggle and run and roll, they bounce and move all over the place. They wiggle when you hold them and they've got such exuberant energy that when they enter a room you notice. They like to touch and taste everything. And they can look you in the eye with such charming honesty that for a second you don't know for sure what to do. There are so many things to be tickled about. Washing those sticky little fingers and soft little chins can bring a smile to any sourpuss.

Life is full of the ridiculous, and children have a knack for seeing it everywhere. Four-year-old Annie was the smartest little girl. An adult asked her one day, "Do you have a boyfriend?" She looked at him, ran to her mother's side, started laughing, and answered, "That's a funny question." Then she giggled some more. Mom giggled too because it was a such a silly question.

Giggling starts as a ripple and may expand into a deep belly laugh. It's truly therapeutic, relaxing, and calming. With a little laughter you're free to enjoy the absurd. Kids are quick to laugh, and you don't have to be a comedian to entertain them. Little kids, especially, will laugh at just about anything—just give them an excuse. A silly face or an absurd comment can elicit shrieks of delight, especially coming from you.

Sandy took a van full of third graders to the park. While driving down the road, the kids laughed and waved at the passers-by. Some grouches ignored the kids, but other folks smiled, honked their horns, and waved too; and then the kids laughed louder. If a kid waves at you, wave back; it's a very easy way to spread a lot of happiness around.

Never squelch those giggles. If you find that you haven't felt giddy for a while, try talking gibberish or singing a nonsensical tune to break the ice; the reaction you get from your child will certainly keep the momentum going. And if you have really forgotten how to giggle, invite a team of thirteen-year-old girls to afternoon tea. That will surely get things going in the giggling direction.

Keep Messes in Perspective

❧❧❧

Why is it when kids first begin to walk, as soon as your back is turned they head directly to the toilet bowl and make delightful sounds and chirping noises as they splash the water around? They laugh merrily as they splatter the water on the floor and on the walls, seemingly determined to get the toilet paper soggy and drench the entire room before getting caught. Their little arms and legs shake with glee as they watch you freak out. You're convinced they'll get sick with some sort of exotic disease or infection but of course they never do.

Perhaps this is a good reminder that our children's happiness is more important than an immaculate house. I remember one day when I had I scrubbed the kitchen floor and Manda came running with muddy feet, saying, "Mommy, Mommy, come see the kitty." I put down my mop and went to see the kitty. Manda looked up and smiled at me and I did not care about the muddy floor.

Although it is true that I prefer my house neat, over the years I've discovered that messes don't matter so much—it's how you handle them. Manda's bedroom was such a shambles that I sometimes called it a pigsty. In desperation I made a rule that if she would keep a path clear to her bed and shut the door, she could have her room any way she liked. We called her decorating style "creative clutter," but even with the door closed, her room still bothered me. So I started saying, "I'd really appreciate you thinking about cleaning up your room," or "I'm looking forward to the day when you clean up your room." Well, I was patient, and thirteen years later she cleaned up her room; now if you were to come for a visit, you would see that she has the neatest room in the house. Moral of the story: being messy as a child isn't necessarily a permanent disorder.

Use your energy to create a home where things are happening. A home that is cozy and lived-in is a happier place for active families. Friends won't feel uptight when dropping by to visit if they know you are relaxed about how the house looks. You can keep the messes in perspective when you remember that one of these days the kids will be gone and you'll have the house all to yourself, and may sigh wistfully at the thought of those wet towels on the bathroom floor.

Enjoy Dinner Together

Throughout the ages the dinnertime ritual has signified family and community bonding. Nowadays it seems almost a lost art, replaced by meals on the run. With both parents working long hours and kids on the go, family dinners have fallen by the wayside. But when schedules allow, meals together can be a joyful time of talking, listening, and sharing—even if it's over fast food.

Try to bring the entire family together at regular intervals for a common meal, even if it's only once a week. Make a date with the rest of the family, and see that it's kept. You could take turns making each kid's "favorite" and Mom's and Dad's too and always feature a special treat for dessert or a movie-and-popcorn fest afterward. Once the family night becomes a habit, you may well find it's the highlight of the week for everyone!

I once knew a family who often gathered around their piano and sang before supper. Sometimes they sang right through dessert. Dinners with them were true occasions, somewhat unusual but certainly memorable.

Even if your meals aren't quite so festive, at least avoid tension. Dinnertime should not be an occasion for confrontations or lectures on manners—no one can digest food when angry or afraid. Family closeness and communication is far more important than etiquette. Reserve the serious discussions for a more appropriate place and time, and never use this occasion to reprimand or scold. Let your dinnertime be one of sharing and coming together, a time for checking in and keeping in touch.

Consider a family "cook-off" once a month, where each family member contributes one dish and invites one friend. Or get to know your neighbors and share some meals together. Our neighbors, the Hansens, have a such a knack for informally including us at their mealtime, that we don't like to go too long now without dropping by to see what's cooking. Everyone can contribute, young children too—even a three year old can set the table. And everyone can help clean up; adults, especially women, do not need to do all the work. Mike always makes cleaning up the kitchen fun. He learned it growing up in a large family of boys, where everyone did their own dishes and one pan before they were excused. It was as natural as brushing his teeth each morning, and now his kids are doing the same.

One family solved the who-is-going-to-cook problem by having simple meals on workdays. They might serve rice and vegetables in pretty bowls to be eaten with chopsticks, or baked potatoes with many kinds of toppings. Whatever they cook, they prepare it lovingly.

Family dinners are meant to provide nourishment for both body and soul. Add candles or flowers to the table, serve dinner with a grateful heart, and you'll surely have a heavenly meal.

Brag About Them

Children thrive on heartfelt praise and recognition from their loved ones, and those who grow up knowing they are valued and enjoyed are more receptive to love; they are comfortable with positive feedback and they can give and receive affection naturally and easily. Some children grow up never hearing honest words of love from their parents. They are suspicious of compliments and uncomfortable with positive recognition; they lack self-esteem. Children who are accustomed to constant negativity in the home have difficulty accepting the slightest praise; they get anxious and nervous, as though they are unable to let love in.

A child needs to hear that you enjoy being her parent. Clara told me, "My mom likes me so much, she can't stop bragging." Tell your children how much you love them, but also tell them how much you enjoy having them as part of your life, using language they understand: "You and baby sister and Daddy are my favorites!" "You're my best boy!" "Nobody can take your place in my heart." If all they ever hear are your complaints, they'll be confused and wonder if you even like being a parent.

Some parents brag only when the child is not around, because they don't want the child to get a "swelled head" or become "conceited." But conceited people are merely trying to overcompensate for feelings of inadequacy. I recommend honest praise about your children, to them and in front of them. Don't worry about it "going to their heads"; they seem to keep it all in balance, and I've never heard of a child being "spoiled" by loving praise from a parent. I once showed to a friend a water color painting of Manda's which I'd had matted. He said, "Those are beautiful, Manda. You are a fine artist." "Nope," she said. "I'm just a silly painter."

Children especially need to know that you're proud of them when they have failed. "Congratulations for hanging in there," Scott reassuringly told Michael, who had come in last in his first thirty-two-meter run. Tell them when you are proud of their effort: "You showed a lot of courage; I'm proud of you for trying so hard." Be sure to make the distinction between failing at some task and being a failure: "I know you feel discouraged, but I am *so* proud of you for giving it your best!" Even when the recital ends with a resounding thud, a dejected eight-year-old deserves a banana split for finishing the piece *and* for all those afternoons spent practicing.

When the Thompsons took their two children to meet distant relatives for the first time, the relatives remarked about how polite the children were. Tom said in front of the kids, "We think our kids are really neat people." Riding home in the car he said to them, "I really like you both." Just as plants soak up water, your children need your loving words, and with them they will thrive.

Generate Family Festivals

Family festivals, celebrations, and rituals are opportunities to come and turn an ordinary day into one to remember. Celebrations strengthen the bonds between the ones you love, reinforce those things you have in common, and establish traditions that will live on, even after the children are grown. It doesn't matter whether your family is made up of two, ten, or eighty, a family festival will draw you closer. Rituals marking even seemingly insignificant events—Janey got her braces off, Joe passed his math test—when done in a spirit of gladness bring satisfaction and joy to the home.

You can have as many celebrations as you like. They can be simple or fancy, planned or unplanned. They can be incorporated into everyday life or take place once a year. Brandon and his father don't talk much, but every summer they make several trips to their favorite fishing hole—a special tradition they would never skip. The Carters have "ice cream night" every time one of the kids loses a tooth.

You can come together for birthday parties, impromptu get-togethers, or to honor the milestones in life. You don't even need an excuse—just the desire to be together. The Wicks have lots of small family rituals: Amy's dad, Fred, walks to the bakery almost every morning to bring her a fresh bagel. They attend the professional basketball games each season with her older brother and his wife, and each night Fred says a prayer with her. Amy added, "He's so cheerful, I don't know what I'd do without him."

What are your family traditions? What rituals and celebrations bring you joy? Do some need to be added or updated? Chloe and her sister, Alice, and their mother have a new ritual: since they live in different states, once a month they talk on a conference call. The Hatch family decided to redo their traditional Thanksgiving; the parents and their two children now volunteer to serve dinner at a shelter. You also might want to change the way you celebrate other holidays or birthdays. One year Manda and I had a white twig covered with lights for our Christmas tree. That marked the beginning of our effort to make our holidays less commercial.

A family festival centers around the joy of being kindred spirits, of knowing each other, and of sharing lives. To generate a family festival requires only your commitment to gatherings filled with honest, heartfelt interaction. Getting together out of obligation is merely a dull routine; but coming together to celebrate one another is fun, meaningful, and deeply fulfilling. A family event with heart, gratitude, and mutual appreciation is indeed a glorious occasion.

Thank Them for the Little Things

Saying thank you to your child and acknowledging all her contributions to your family life is a modest yet magical way to motivate kids. It works so well, in fact, I'm astonished that more parents don't do it. It's a fact that when someone notices the little things you do, you are more willing to keep on doing them. Honestly expressing your appreciation is not only gracious in itself, it instills graciousness in your child.

Thank your child cheerfully for bringing in the mail or answering the phone. Lisa told her four-year-old daughter, "Thanks for hanging up your towel; that really helps me a lot." Carly beamed, and her mother never mentioned that the towel was crooked. Holly, age five, was watching her dad wash the car, then she grabbed a rag and started following him around, washing and rubbing. He encouraged her: "Holly, you are such a willing helper!"

No matter how insignificant the act may seem, be sure to thank your child for her contributions—putting her laundry in the basket, picking up her toys, or not interrupting you while you were on the phone. A child who lives with constant criticism will grow to feel incompetent and unimportant; he will start finding fault with others and condemn himself. Whereas a child whose efforts are continually acknowledged will develop a healthy sense of self-confidence and capability. Even if the made-up bed is rather lumpy, praise the accomplishment.

Remember, periodic rewards are most effective for keeping a child motivated. Children, like all people, respond to recognition; so even if your child receives an allowance for chores, it's a good idea to give an occasional bonus: either money or a special treat. Praise and thanks maintain friendly relations and will energize your child to keep on contributing, knowing that his efforts are noted and appreciated.

For the Lopez family, Saturday morning is chore time, followed by a fast-food lunch of the kids' choice. The parents told me, "We work as a team to get the job done, and then we party together at lunch." Remembering the thank-yous will keep your kids pulling together as willing contributors to get the household tasks done. In such a climate you'll all be whistling while you work.

Esprit

*When you let the love of a child
transform your heart,
you are renewed.*

Focus on the Joy They Bring

Parenting is hard but children are a joy. When you love a child, it changes you! You have a new focus. When you become a mother or father, you have a new role and a new responsibility. Fortunately parenting is a two-way street—you walk together, and as you take them by the hand, they take you by the heart. You give to them and they give to you. And although parenting is demanding, intriguing, frustrating, frightening, and confusing, children are joyful, entertaining, enlightening, and heartwarming. We show them the ways of the world, and they show us the ways of the heart. We try to love them unconditionally, then we forget, and make demands. We want them to succeed, we push and have expectations, but, even so, our children forgive us and love us unconditionally. And with that innocent forgiveness you come to understand that the proof of God's grace can been seen in the forgiving nature of your child.

You can choose to focus on the difficulty or on the joy, but when you concentrate on the special delights, the little heart-melting moments of raising a child, you realize what a magnificent path you have chosen. To give birth to a child is biology, but to love a child is divine. In a sense, with a child in your life, you are in partnership with the Almighty, for you are entrusted with the care of a soul.

Some people believe that children choose their parents and although I don't know if this is so, it's an intriguing thought that such an innocent soul would choose you for his mother or father. When you think of it in this way you realize that parenthood is a blessing. Together you and your child are carving a life; by helping your child grow into a beautiful human being, you are giving something of immense value to humanity and all of us are enriched.

Your role as parent is significant and far reaching because your child's life will carry the fragrance of you for years to come; just as your life has touched many, so will the life of your child. Take your role as parent joyously, and if you find yourself feeling burdened, remind yourself that your love is the foundation on which your child will grow into a healthy adult— we all know that the future generations will need healthy, love-filled, grown-up people running the show.

Children are gifts from God. Appreciate them, be glad they are a part of your life, and recognize the honor and miracle that has been bestowed upon you. If you know a child, you are blessed. They are radiant, tender beings of light. They may be expensive, but when you nurture the soul of a child, you are gaining heavenly riches.

Believe in Possibilities

❦ ❦ ❦

A newborn baby comes into the world as a bundle of energy, full of pure potential—a fresh, new spirit. Such a little body, such a big miracle. Regina, mother to two, told me, "You can't mold kids. I thought they were blank sheets of paper. Boy, was I shocked." When you recognize that your children have their own destiny and their own divine nature, when you trust that this is so, endless possibilities for spiritual comfort will come to you.

As parents we have a tendency to think it's our role to guide our children toward worldly success, and although this is partially true, it is not the entire picture. Your children are spiritual beings; their souls as well as their bodies need your care. Parents who put the emphasis on things—success, fame, possessions, and worldly thrills—are doing their children a great disservice. I met Luke in a hospital emergency room after he tried to kill himself with pills and booze. He was a good student, was accepted to college, and had every material advantage; still he was miserable. This is not an unusual story, for our children are bombarded daily with worldly seductions that slowly corrode their souls.

Believing in possibilities means trusting in the divine nature of your child and seeing the divine nature in yourself. Parents can light the way to deeper fulfillment in little ways, the most important of which is by your example. Live more simply, treat every living thing lovingly, learn to live in the moment, and take time to enjoy the things in life that truly matter. Spend time with your children in nature. Whether or not you go to church, you can add a spiritual practice to your life. Tom takes his family on a retreat to the desert to feel the connection between the earth and the universe—sleeping under the stars refreshes us all in ways that are hard to describe. Nick and Satya meditate. The Hogans have a family pea patch in the middle of their city. The Wongs sing in the choir, the Joneses belong to a prayer group, and Manda and I put out a daily offering of flowers at our front door.

A vital part of our spiritual quest is coping with the down times, the hard times, the turmoil, the anguish. Children too feel blue and feel the longings of their souls. As parents we sometimes jump in too quickly to make it all right. Sometimes it is wiser to be with them in spirit and let the answers unfold. Believing in possibilities, we know that although tough times come, we can transcend them and survive. That with each struggle, comes a lesson and a fresh possibility.

Open Up to the Miracle of Transformation

❀ ❀ ❀

Children touch your heart in ways you cannot predict—a child will change you inside out and introduce you to a new dimension of your spiritual being. They will bring new adventure, new people, new ideas, new feelings, joys, and sorrows into your life. They will take you to places inside your soul you may never have known before. This can be an enlightening, blessed journey if you open your heart and remain vulnerable, but if your heart is closed and your mind locked tightly in a rigid mind-set, you are going to have many struggles and not much success. When you remain open to all the wonderful miracles of transformation, life with your child will become deeply fulfilling.

My experience is that most parents reach adulthood with some emotional scars of their own. Staying open to your children will give you the opportunity to heal the wounds of your own childhood. Here's an example: When Cindy's daughter was two years old, Cindy came to the painful realization that her own parents never spent time with her at night. Instead she had been sent off to bed night after night, alone, fearful, and crying. One evening while reading a bedtime story to her daughter, she remembered her loneliness at night and her longing for her mother's comfort. For the first time she understood her fear of the dark. By allowing herself to be open to her child and to her own wounded heart, she was able to heal this long-repressed memory. With this recognition came the transformation of fear to understanding.

Stay open, listen closely, and you will learn about yourself too. You will come to know yourself well enough that you can make sensible choices about what is right for your family. Being open does not mean drifting aimlessly. Being open means considering all the options before you decide. Talk to other parents and see how they are coping, but never follow their advice blindly—listen to your intuition and trust yourself to know what's right for you and your child. Being open to transformation means that you will conscientiously search for answers within your own heart. When you let the love of a child transform you, you have become rich, you are renewed.

Remember That They Have Not Been on the Earth Very Long

❧❧❧

Sometimes we forget that the children have just arrived on the earth, and we expect way too much, way too soon. We become impatient, urging them to learn it all, know it all, and "act their age," whatever that means.

Although it is true that children learn quickly about life by observation, it is unrealistic to expect them to be on top of it all and always get it right. Keith and Cicely's three children were two, four, and six when they realized that their expectations for the oldest were unfair. One evening after they referred to her as "our big girl," she responded with, "I wish I was your baby."

When you find yourself beginning every sentence with "Don't," stop and ask yourself, "Have I explained what I *do* want? Have I showed him how to shut the door softly? Have I explained how to get my attention when I'm busy?" Explaining the *dos* works much better than constantly harping on the *don'ts*. Try this three-time teaching and practice formula: share information three times in three different ways.

When Marilee heard herself yelling at her two boys, "Don't be so

116

rough with the kittens," she realized that she had never taught them how to hold the kittens properly. With that she stopped and showed them: "Hold the kittens gently, with both hands. Put them down slowly. Pat their fur this way." She let them practice, then showed them three more times, and after a while they got the hang of it.

Josh was very frustrated that his son Clay resisted using the potty. Clay was having lots of accidents, and Josh had resorted to threatening which only made things worse. One day, Josh's mother observed this battle and said to Josh, "I had the same trouble with you." Immediately Josh understood that the pressure he had felt as a child, he was now putting on his own son. Josh changed his approach right away, reminding himself that Clay had been practicing using the potty for only a brief five weeks.

Give your children lots of practice time for whatever they're learning, and remind yourself that, after all, they've been here a very short time.

Marvel at How
They Are Growing

Isn't it incredible how quickly children grow? Only yesterday they were in diapers, and now they are going to the first grade, and the next minute they're teenagers. They are so capable and independent that it's easy to forget that they haven't mastered everything.

For example, many parents assume that teenagers feel confident and understand all the steps for getting a job when, in fact, most teenagers are quite nervous about the whole process. Although they aren't quick to let you know it, they very well may need your direction. So instead of saying, "Don't be so lazy—get a job," you might try teaching them the steps for finding a job and sharing some of your experiences. Then give them time to think it over. Thinking it over is a kind of mental practice—an important first step before taking action.

Jim gave his son Grant quite a boost when he suggested that Grant collect written recommendations from teachers to attach to his job applications. Although Grant didn't get going right away (teens rarely do), Jim made the suggestion a few more times. Grant obviously gave it some thought, because he gathered the recommendations and earned quite an edge when he got up his nerve to apply.

As children grow there will be many times when they reject your help even though they need it. That's all right—it's just another way of learning. The biggest challenge for you as parents is to avoid saying "I told you so." Jesse was cooking dinner for his friends and his mom was only trying to be helpful when she said, "Don't overcook the halibut." He insisted, "I can do it." He never mentioned it again, but the very next time he cooked for friends, he asked her, "How long should I cook the pasta?" Isn't it amazing how they grow?

When in doubt about what they know, put yourself in their place. It has taken us years of practice to master what works and what doesn't, and still there are many times when we stumble. Be patient and guide them gently, allowing them to learn from their own mistakes. Marvel at how they are growing. Remember that they are finding their way.

Let Them Help

From a young age, children want to help and be active participants in family life. They want to make a contribution, they want to belong. Your willingness to let them help out in the way they desire will teach them to exercise judgment, take responsibility for themselves, and make meaningful choices.

We all hope that our children will grow up to be responsible adults, able to care for their own needs. We want them to have happy, independent, and satisfying lives. How do we do this? Some parents believe that to instill a sense of responsibility, they must, above all else, demand a high level of dedicated participation around the house and at school. They think that good grades, clean rooms, and obediently doing chores are a sign of a responsible child, and that messy rooms, poor grades, and pouty attitudes mean the child is not learning responsibility. But that is not necessarily so.

In order to take responsibility for his own life, a child must first have the opportunity to exercise control over his life. This is the only way he learns to make choices and live with the consequences of his choices. When a parent always tells the child what to do without allowing him any input, the child becomes more and more dependent on others and less confident in his own ability to make decisions for himself.

Ask your children what they would like to do to contribute to the household, and let them know what would be helpful. Suggest a few projects, and let them make a choice. When asked by his mother what chore he would be willing to do, Jeff, eight years old, said he didn't want to do the same thing every week but wanted to choose each Monday. After several weeks of choosing, he decided that created too much pressure and chose a more permanent chore. The most valuable lesson he learned was not from doing the job, but from being actively involved in the decision making.

When they are young, keep the chores simple. At age three, Ellie helps water the plants and Clementine feeds the cats. At age four, Davey puts the clean silverware in the drawer, and five-year-old Shelly chose picking up everyone's dirty clothes and putting them in the laundry. As they grow you can let them do more, but don't demand perfection or blind obedience. At eleven years old, Rick sometimes does his own laundry. Keep things flexible and you will create an environment where your children will willingly help out and learn solid values in the process.

Cherish the Innocence

Have you ever held a sleeping baby in your arms? Felt a baby curl its tiny hand around your finger? Heard those gurgling coos of contentment? Did you ever change a diaper of a squirming, laughing baby? Has a baby patted your cheek and pulled at your nose? If so, you are blessed, for you have been touched by innocence.

Babies grow so fast. Soon they are walking, pulling the books down from the shelves, and jumping on your bed. Next thing you know, they're catching bugs in jars and selling lemonade from a stand. Just discovering something new pleases and amazes them.

But it's not just babies. If you have ever heard the voices of a first-grade choir, your heart swelled up so big you thought it might burst. And you've probably experienced a child saying something so straightforward, so truthful, that you're stunned. Such purity catches you off-guard, and for a moment you know you're feeling the presence of the divine. Perhaps that is why parents walk with such pride on graduation night or cry at their child's wedding. And perhaps that is why the smell of baby powder floods your brain with memories that you can't even put into words.

There is a biblical saying, "and a little child shall lead them," which suggests that such blessed innocence can point the way. We all have known adults who seem to expect the worst; they are cynical, sarcastic, and wary of others. They don't trust anyone and are out only for themselves. They too were once innocent babies, but they lost their innocence on the way to maturity. Our children are exposed to too much too soon—we push them to grow up and we deprive them of a childhood. With so much glitz and glamour plastered everywhere, it seems as though our whole society is anti-children and anti-innocence. A shift in emphasis is badly needed, and we can start in our own homes.

To me the truly grown-up people aren't those jaded by "maturity" but rather the ones who have kept the innocence alive in their own hearts. They have a sparkle in their eyes and spring in their step. Just being around such a person lifts you up; you feel happy and inspired. Grandpa Simon was like that—kids of all ages hung around him. He gave them hard candy from his pockets and let everyone pet his rabbits. He grew raspberries and he'd feed you toast and jam. He knew when to talk and when to keep quiet. He told stories that made you feel better even though you weren't feeling bad.

Respect the mature innocence in grown-up people you know and, whenever you can, look into the eyes of a child so you might catch a glimpse of theirs.

Listen for the
Spiritual Language

Children are innately spiritual, and if you pay close attention they can speak to you about the subtle energies of another dimension; whether or not you believe, it can be intriguing to listen to what they have to say. Children's intuition is highly attuned, and frequently they hear and see things that we miss, as they aren't so tightly immersed in "reality" yet. At age five, Heidi said people were surrounded by colorful clouds of light. At age four, Rosie had two imaginary playmates who held her hands wherever she went. She gave them strange names which her mother found out later were actual French words. Elliot, at age four and a half, told his father, "White Eagle taught me to swing—just look at a place in the sky, send your thoughts through it, and you'll swing." At age five, Ryder told his mom, "Everyone has an angel." Before about age six, children are highly attuned to the spiritual world and with things unseen and unspoken, but they are more than likely to lose touch once they start school and are exposed to traditional thinking and logical reasoning. Until then they are adept at tuning in to our thoughts. For example, Marie, the mother of three, was thinking about death one day, wondering what word she could use in place of *dying*. At just that moment her little daughter Laura walked into the room and said, "How about saying *passing on*, Mom?" This certainly made her notice, since she hadn't said a word out loud!

Children have highly developed intuition—they can feel the energy and vibes of others. Sometimes just seeing somebody will cause a child to start crying loudly; she moves to avoid that person and, although she can't put into words why, she can feel the person's energy and wants to stay away. Trust this instinct in your child.

Some children already know profound spiritual truths without ever being taught. Jody, at age four, told her ailing grandfather, "When you die, Grandpa, you'll just move someplace else." Part of honoring your child's divine nature is recognizing her spiritual language and respecting her special perceptions.

Build Family-Friendly Neighborhoods

❧❧❧

Because raising a child is such a complicated process, you need lots of other people in your life, including grandparents, baby-sitters, a family doctor, neighbors, teachers, coaches, friends, and advisers. You can raise a child alone, but it's so much easier with a listening ear or a helping hand from others like you who want the best for all our children and who understand that we must pull together to create neighborhoods and communities that are family-friendly. We all struggle from time to time, and when the whole community pulls together, it's not only easier, it makes all of our lives better. Many people are recognizing in this fast-paced, achievement-oriented, technology-manipulated world that simple kindness, togetherness, understanding, and fellowship are fuel for the soul we all can use.

Family-friendly communities value children and emphasize creating environments and services that ensure that each family thrives. You can't wait for someone else to do it—you must get active to make things happen for your children. Here is the best place to start:

First, get to know your neighbors. When I struggled as a single parent, my community of family, friends, and neighbors came to my aide in so many ways. When Manda was just a toddler, the Levells fed her night after night when I had to work late; the Hansens, whom I can still call in a pinch, opened their doors to us; the Fishers (the best baby-sitting family in the world) loved Manda as if she were their own, and Kathy Jean went far beyond the duties of an aunt by teaching her to drive a stick shift.

Next, get to know your children's friends and their parents, meet your child's teachers, join in the local activities, know who is running the community, and who is making the decisions that affect family life. Then let others know what you think and how you want your community to function. Speak up. Get involved. Join the PTSA, volunteer at school, or start a family-friendly community project—you can make a difference.

Children want to learn about the world outside their own backyards and they want to make a contribution. Bryan, nine years old, told his parents, "I want to help the homeless." With his parents' backup he launched his first "Warm-Up Campaign" to collect blankets for street people.

Reaching out to others puts our priorities in perspective, and helps us to appreciate the comforts of home which we so often take for granted. When we open our hearts to others, we show our children that we share this planet with so many other folks just like us. When we reach out to each other, we find that we are more alike than we are different. Getting to know the people in your community makes the whole place friendlier—and that's good for every family.

Let Go When It's Time

❧❧❧

Letting go does not begin when your children turn eighteen or twenty-one and box up their stuff and move out. It begins in many little ways even when they are as young as two or three. Many a parent has sent a child off to school for the first time, waving good-bye at the bus stop and crying buckets of tears. Many parents have felt pain as they watched the coach keep their child sitting on the bench.

Opportunities for letting go continue throughout a lifetime, and it almost always hurts. Not only do we want to protect our children from all the unfairness and pain, but we also want to share in their happiness and glory. Sometimes they choose to share it with someone other than you. Becky made the cutest clown costume for her five-year-old Meg and was stunned when Meg insisted on going trick-or-treating with the neighbors instead of her. Matt was honored on local television for an act of bravery, and his parents wanted to take him out to dinner. But after the show he said, "See you later—I'm going out with my friends."

Letting go means watching as your children make their own way in the world without you. Letting go means loosening your grip and your tendency to control. It means letting them make their own mistakes and their own decisions. Letting go is remembering that your children are not yours forever, but are gifts shared for a time. Some parents hold on too tightly; others don't get involved enough. Finding the balance can be tricky, but if you listen carefully, they will guide you: "Look, Mom, I cut my hair." "Dad, can I walk to the store?" "Mom, I'm going to ride my bike to town—see you later." "Mom, I'm getting my belly-button pierced." "Dad, I've decided to backpack through Europe with my boyfriend."

Each of these milestones offers a new challenge. How much you loosen your grip of course depends on your child's age and the circumstances, but you will nevertheless come face-to-face with such challenges almost every day of your child's life. Your three year old wants to play in the backyard by herself. Can your ten year old spend the day at the mall with friends? Go to the late show at the movies? What about staying out all night on prom night? "Mom, can I borrow the car?"

Jayne and Dave wanted Marc to play in the backyard but he preferred the park across the street. They wanted him to go college close by; he went to Japan on a exchange and stayed, then he married a girl from Holland and now he lives there.

As they assert more independence, that you will experience a loss is a given, but you can rest assured knowing you have loved them enough to let go. Kaye, the mother of three grown children, told me, "When you finally know your children are happy, you are never alone."

Let Them Come Back

When your children are young you are actively involved in directing their lives, but as they grow and eventually move out, your role shifts to standing by just in case they need you. It's paradoxical, but when you give your children the freedom to make their own way in the world, to live their lives fully, they'll be more likely to come back to share their lives with you. When they know they can come and go without feeling guilty, they'll enjoy hanging out with you more and want to know how you're doing. Sometimes they'll surprise you and ask for your input.

That's because, just as children want the freedom to explore beyond their own family, they also want to belong, they want to know that they have the security of a cozy home and a loving family who will be there through thick and thin, no matter what: "I'm scared; can I sleep with you?" "I'll get homesick so I'm not going to summer camp again." "Mom, come get me—I don't want to spend the night here." "Maybe I can come over on Sunday to do my laundry?" "Can I come home for the summer."

As they head out into the world, you will be giving your children a great advantage if they know you will be there to listen, to understand, to provide the security of a loving home in which they can re-charge their batteries and get going once again.

Even as an adult you probably feel comforted knowing your parents are there for you, knowing that, in a pinch, you could turn to them—for advice, a loan, whatever. And if your parents are no longer alive or there for you, you are keenly aware of what you are missing and how you don't want your own children to feel such a loss. When your children know they have you on their side, they feel a lot more secure in the world, trusting they can turn to you for assistance. Give your children the blessing of life-long connection by letting them know you will always be there whenever they are in need of a home, a shoulder, or just a good, hot meal. With you as their biggest supporter saying: "Mi casa es su casa," they'll know that you'll always welcome their calls or their visits, and all of you will benefit.

Show Them Compassion
and Ask for Theirs

❧❧❧

I would like to tell you a true story about compassion. A financially strapped single mother I know was having a very bad week. She had locked her keys in the car, learned that her youngest needed braces, forgotten an important meeting, and, to top it off, her oldest daughter spilled ketchup on the brand-new couch. Well, that was the final straw! She started screaming and scolding her girls. Her two daughters, as children sometimes do, began talking back, pointing out their mother's weaknesses: "You're always upset . . . you overreact . . . you're so unreasonable. . . ."

Suddenly the mother stopped in the middle of defending herself and said, "You're right—I've been very upset lately." Then she asked, "Will you show me a little TLC? I need a dose of compassion."

Her oldest daughter replied, "How can I show you compassion when you're acting so weird?"

To that the mother responded, "That's when I really need it. It's easy to show compassion when I'm okay and behaving myself, but giving me TLC when I've blown it, messed up, or let you down is what compassion's all about. So will you both try to understand that things are tough for me right now?" Nothing more was said that night, but she could feel that something had changed for them all. Since then they have been treating one another with more tenderness.

As a body needs food, a soul needs compassion. Loving your children without compassion is not enough. Compassion is a soft and gentle understanding—it's tender loving care. It means you are attuned, that you really feel for another. It's noticing the look on another's face that says, "I'm really having a bad day." Three-year-old Millie had been shopping with her mother all day and was tired of sitting in the stroller, so she crawled out and ran down the aisle. When her mother picked her up, she screamed and kicked so loudly that heads turned to see what was going on. Even though her mother was embarrassed by all the commotion, she understood that shopping is really hard on little ones, so she comforted Millie with a hug and let her walk by her side.

Children need a generous dose of compassion when they are tired, cranky, or just plain impossible, and so do you. Take notice when they are out of sorts and tell them when you're having a rough time, too, then pour on the tenderness.

Protect All Our Children

※ ※ ※

As parents we want to protect our children from all the pain and injustices of life. That, of course, is impossible, but we *can* create an environment where children are physically, emotionally, and spiritually safe. And we will do a much better job of protecting them when we think of all the children in the world as our responsibility.

All children need our protection from the many forms of abuse—the verbal put-downs, name calling, physical punishment, and beatings. Some children suffer from a lack of love and others are the victims of poverty. We can and should make it our business to protect children from the tyranny of parents and other adults who, because of their inability or unwillingness to heal their own personal pain, inflict their rage on helpless children.

Let's put our energies where it truly matters. John and Heather met Angie when she was six years old. Her mother, a single parent, had just been diagnosed with a serious illness and was unable to care for Angie. John and Heather took Angie and her mother under their wing. They cared for Angie and brought her mother to their home, where she died with Angie at her side. For seventeen years they nurtured, encouraged, and supported Angie. She calls them, "My guardian-angel parents."

In cities and communities across our country, there are children in need of guardian angels. We can begin today in small ways to make enormous differences in the lives of such children. Together we can find a way to protect children everywhere from hunger, disease, and violence.

Wally sponsored a struggling young man with anonymous financial assistance throughout his school years. Phil has become a mentor to four young men; he understands that now, more than ever, children need adult role models who actively take a personal interest in their lives. By spending time with them at work as well as play, Phil is giving them a view of life they would otherwise miss.

You, too, can make a difference if you will only take a stand. Did a child go hungry in your neighborhood last night? Did one sleep in the street behind a garbage can? Was a child slapped and ridiculed? Was a child shot? Did you speak up or did you look the other way? Did you pretend not to notice? Is the water and air too polluted to raise a healthy child? Will the earth be green for their tomorrows?

It is a lot to think about, it is a heavy responsibility, and there is much work to be done. But the solutions, the responsibility, and the work are ours—we brought these children into the world and it is our responsibility to care for them. Who will if we don't? You will make the world a better place when you become an advocate for a child; when you protect just one, you are a guardian angel.

Keep Them in Your Hearts
and in Your Prayers

❧❧❧

Once you love a child he will have a place in your heart forever. Your children touch you so deeply that not a moment goes by when you aren't aware of them, feeling their presence within you, their faces permanently etched in your mind. They are so much a part of your being that if something ever happened to them, the best part of you would die too. If you could, you'd control everything and watch them at every turn; you want to keep them safe from harm, but you know there is only so much you can do. You have taught them what they need to know; you've tried to prepare them as best you could.

Sometimes you feel so helpless, knowing there is nothing more that you can do. You can't lock them up, or hide them away, so what else can you do but pray? Pray for them moment to moment and day to day that they might walk in the light with joy and peace. Ask God to watch over them. Say a simple prayer, straight from your heart. The spiritual connection is always there between you and your child; when you pray, you'll be linking up through the spiritual airwaves. Whether they are going next door or miles away, a prayer will help when your precious child is out of your sight, beyond your reach.

Never ever leave them feeling angry or hurt—always patch things up. Tell them, "I am always with you even though we are separated—I am loving you and thinking of you, for I hold you in my heart." And as you hold them in your heart, remember that they love you too, they feel your presence, and want you to be happy and safe. They want the best for you, and while you are praying for them, they are probably praying for you.

Judy Ford, MSW, has been a therapist, public speaker, and human relations consultant for the past twenty years. Her parenting classes, *Parenting with Love and Laughter*, give parents practical tools to use while focusing on the joy of parenting. In addition to her seminars, Judy frequently speaks on the power of love and laughter to enrich both our professional and personal lives. For information on her seminars, write:

P.O. Box 834
Kirkland, WA 98083

Judy Ford and daughter, Manda

If you liked *Wonderful Ways To Love a Child*, chances are you'll enjoy Conari Press' other titles. Our goal is to publish books that will positively impact people's lives and further our individual and collective growth. Call or write for a catalog:

Conari Press
1144 65th Street, Suite B
Emeryville, CA 94608
(800) 685-9595